D1637107

$ 24.20

ADVOCACY
VIEWS FROM THE BENCH

ADVOCACY
VIEWS FROM THE BENCH

ROBERT F. REID
AND
RICHARD E. HOLLAND
OF THE SUPREME COURT OF ONTARIO

1984
CANADA LAW BOOK INC.
240 EDWARD STREET, AURORA, ONTARIO

© 1984 Robert F. Reid and Richard E. Holland

All rights reserved. No part of this book may be reproduced in any form by any photographic, electronic, mechanical or other means, or used in any information storage and retrieval system, without the written permission of the publisher.

The quotations from *The Autobiography of Sir Patrick Hastings* on pages 7 and 20 are printed with the permission of William Heinemann Ltd., London, England.

The quotation from *The Art of Cross-Examination*, 4th ed., by Francis L. Wellman (Copyright 1923, 1926 by Macmillan Publishing Co. Inc., renewed 1951, 1964 by Ethel Wellman) on page 28 is printed with the permission of Macmillan Publishing Co., New York.

Canadian Cataloguing in Publication Data

Reid, Robert F., 1923-
   Advocacy, views from the bench

Includes index.
ISBN 0-88804-024-5.

1. Practice of law — Canada.   2. Trial practice —
Canada.   I. Holland, Richard E. (Richard
Estcourt), 1925-   . II. Title.

KE335.R45 1984   347.71'0504   C84-099723-X

FOREWORD

I have had the advantage of reading in advance this informative and frequently humorous book by Mr. Justice Robert F. Reid and Mr. Justice Richard E. Holland who had wide experience when they were at the Bar and have presided over many trials in the Supreme Court of Ontario.

As the learned authors properly point out, judges who are subjected to the persuasive efforts of counsel are in the very best position to observe the frailties and the strengths of advocacy techniques used by counsel.

The book is really two books. The first Part deals broadly with matters which some of us have thought about but no one has written about, using, as the authors do, anecdotes and actual incidents which have occurred during trials to illustrate their points. This Part covers such subjects as "How to Learn Advocacy", "Know the Rules" and "Winning and Losing". One very interesting chapter is "Court Room Choreography" dealing with where counsel should stand at various stages of a trial and the distracting movements of counsel. Another chapter is self-explanatory from its title, "How to Tell the Pros from the Dabblers". Other chapters cover court room manners, court room dress and the traditions and customs of the Bar. One chapter I read with great interest was on objectionable personal mannerisms in court. When I read it I said to myself, and I will not specify the mannerism I had in mind, "I've done that", so from now on I am going to be very careful not to do it.

The authors warn counsel to keep one's face straight when disaster occurs in the cross-examination and, as might be expected, they emphasize the importance of speaking up. There is also a chapter on how to handle the rare rude judge and "the take-over judge".

The second Part of the book deals in detail with, among other things, preparation of documents for discovery, pre-trial and trial and the point is made that failure to do the paper work means that the techniques available to counsel at the trial cannot be used effectively. As they say, "Paper may be the bane of counsel, but disorganized paper may be the death of the case for counsel and the client". This chapter is very instructive as to the manner in which documents should be copied and indexed and cross-indexed for counsel's trial brief.

The opening of a case by counsel is discussed in detail and contains many valuable suggestions. There are chapters on examination in chief and cross-examination, including the examination of experts, and I have never read a more informative and helpful discussion of these subjects.

The book has been carefully and gracefully written and contains a mine of useful information. It is obviously required reading for anyone who aspires to be an effective counsel, and for all practising counsel whether they be young, middle-aged or simply old.

John J. Robinette

TABLE OF CONTENTS

PART II
THE ADVOCATE AT TRIAL

ABOUT THIS BOOK

UNTIL THIS BOOK reached its final form these introductory paragraphs were entitled "Preface". Many people who had read the drafts at various stages told us, "No one ever reads Prefaces" but that we should issue a word of warning to readers about the book's rather odd structure. Advice givers are rarely advice takers, but we have taken those words to heart, and modified the Preface into this brief explanation of why we wrote this book and how it acquired its present form.

First, let us say that there are some very good books on advocacy. All were written by successful counsel. That is the tradition and it is natural enough, for advocacy is the craft of persuasion and counsel are the persuaders.

It is odd, however, that little has been heard from the "persuadees", as a late colleague called us: the judges on whom counsel's skills are practised. After all, sitting above the well of the court, with a full view of the play and the players, the judge is in the best possible position to appraise the performance.

The fact is that the view from the Bench is clear and piercing. No amount of time spent at the counsel table can replace the shift in perspective from Bar to Bench. When first experienced, it is startling. Everything is suddenly in a new light. It seems as if everything is revealed and laid bare. You realize that you are no longer an actor: you are the camera.

The quality of advocacy fast becomes the most important thing in your life. The first question judges ask when facing

a difficult trial is, who are the counsel? At the prospect of conducting a trial with inept counsel judges quail. They fear the
unpleasant experience of the trial; they fear also that it will
end badly with an odd or bad result, or even abruptly in a
mistrial. Good trials require good team work. Judges need
good counsel as much as counsel need good judges. Without
an adequate supply of good counsel the system simply will not
work. It is not surprising that when two or three judges are
gathered together in the name of the law, they are probably
discussing counsel.

Between the two of us we have spent almost 70 years at the
Bar and on the Bench. None of the current books on this
acutely important subject, advocacy, was written by a judge.
None describes the view from the Bench. We thought it was
time one did.

That explains why we wrote the book. Now a word about
how it acquired its two-part form. The book is a product of
collaboration but that failed to make it homogeneous. Some
have found an unsettling difference in both the style and the
tone of the two parts. We are aware of that but at an early
point gave up attempting to alleviate it. Each of us is in general
agreement with what the other has said. We have discussed the
contents and revised them at length, but one thing we failed
to master was how to sound like one another. We hope that
the differences will not be found too hard to bear.

The principal responsibility for Part I is Reid's and for
Part II is Holland's. The object of Part I is to pass on to others
things that are not usually found written down in books; the
object of Part II is to help counsel sharpen the tools that they
require to conduct today's increasingly demanding and complicated trials. Many have suggested that readers begin with

Part I and go on to Part II, that is, to move from the general to the particular and so gain a better grasp of what we are trying to accomplish.

Much of what we say is summed up in a few words by one of our former law clerks who read the manuscript. Now a practising barrister, he said:

> From my brief experience in the courts in various capacities, I don't think I have had any insight simpler or more important than that judges are human; they see through most nonsense; they are as different from one another as any group of people; and they are trying as hard as they can to do the just thing. They are above flattery and threats; they have seen good advocacy and bad and good cases and bad. On the whole they can't be fooled, they can only be persuaded.

We believe that our views will generally find agreement among judges, but we do not presume to speak for them all. We hope that our attempt to distil and recount our experience will be of some value to the members of the great profession of law. That would give us great satisfaction, and add another dimension to the pleasure we have had in writing the book.

R.F.R.
R.E.H.

Acknowledgements

To the many who assisted or encouraged us we give our sincere thanks. We are particularly grateful to our colleagues Grange and Krever and to the following members of the Bar who read the manuscript, or parts of it, during its evolution: John D. Honsberger, Q.C., Ronald J. Rolls, Q.C., W. Thomas

McGrenere, Q.C., R. Allan O'Donnell, Q.C., James M. Farley, Q.C., Allan M. Rock, Sandra J. Simpson, E. Eva Frank and Alan J. Pratt.

We could not have hoped for more from a publisher than the assiduous attention given by Alan Marks, who made the editing and production of the book his personal responsibility.

Finally, we are delighted that John J. Robinette, Q.C., the exemplar of advocacy at its best, has honoured us with a Foreword.

R.F.R.
R.E.H.

PART I

DO'S AND DON'TS FOR ADVOCATES

CHAPTER 1

THE ADVOCACY TRADITION IN CANADA

THIS BOOK WAS written principally for those who practise or seek to practise before law courts and administrative tribunals, but it is our hope that it will also be useful to anyone who appears before any person or body that might be swayed by oral presentation. The principles of advocacy do not change, they have merely to be adapted to different circumstances.

The tradition of oral advocacy may have lost ground elsewhere but it remains strong in this country. In the Supreme Court of the United States, we are told, counsel are limited to 30 minutes to present a case. When the time is up a bell rings and they must sit down.

That bell sounds an ominous note. To me, it is a signal that traditional advocacy has failed. As far as we know, there is no such rigid rule or custom in this country, and, with luck and effort, we might never have it. There are occasions when you are expected to work within a time limit, such as on some motions for leave to appeal, but no need has yet been felt for such a limitation on trials or appeals because Canada has enjoyed a fine tradition of skill in advocacy and good advocates do not have to be told when to sit down. Nor, as long as they are assisting the court, do judges wish them to sit down. The bell assumes that no advocate in any case could do anything after 30 minutes but waste time.

If the traditional level of advocacy is maintained we are not likely to need any such rule. Courts, tribunals, boards, committees, councils, commissions, a host of bodies that decide or investigate or recommend, depend on the assistance of skilled advocates and, over the years, they have received it. Advocacy may be in a little trouble at the moment and a few time limits have crept in. So far they have been confined to relatively secondary matters, such as motions for leave, which can by good advocacy be confined without loss, but the ever-increasing demands on the time of courts and tribunals increases the pressure to introduce more of such limitations.

Just as bad advocacy is a time waster, good advocacy is a time saver. Good advocates can strike to the heart of an issue in an interesting and compelling way. They can reduce complexity to rivetting clarity and simplicity. The hearing is alive with excitement and crackling mental energy. The participants are at their best; judges and advocates take part actively in the event. Arguments are modified and adapted to changes as the hearing progresses. Judges can save everyone's time by asking questions to clarify their thinking or to avoid undue extensions of time and effort on points already made or accepted. Written outlines are helpful as a background to oral presentation but they cannot wholly supplant it. When it is well done oral advocacy is both effective and efficient.

Courts try to avoid bad advocacy by attempting to restrict it. They cannot wholly avoid oral hearings but they can cut them off with a time limit and rely on written submissions. Yet in terms of efficiency that can prove a spurious cure, for the volume of the paper seems to increase as the length of the hearing decreases. The water squeezed out of the hearing seems to seep into and swell the paper. There does not appear to be any effective way to limit tonnage. The risk of being swamped arises. Judges become increasingly reliant on assistants. That can take more time than it saves. The process of extracting a decision from a mass of lifeless paper is less efficient and less effective than the process of good oral advocacy.

I hope the day never dawns in Canada when our fine tradition of oral advocacy is lost. My own opinion, based upon my experience in our courts and tribunals, and what I have seen elsewhere, is firm. It is that oral advocacy supplemented by written submissions is by and large more effective and efficient than a process where the real presentation of the case consists of written submissions and oral advocacy is reduced to a formality.

CHAPTER 2

WHY ARE THERE NOT MORE
TOP ADVOCATES?

IF YOU READ many books on advocacy you may be struck
with the reiteration of the view that the quality of advocacy is
falling. It matters not when the book was written; the great
advocates all seem to have slipped into the past and taken the
"art" of advocacy with them.

Whether the general quality of advocacy is falling, or
whether it is high or low, is a matter of individual and highly
subjective appraisal. But I have the very clear impression that
most judges would like to see it raised and many are deeply
concerned that it is not higher.

I am speaking here of the general level; individual skills
vary widely. There are simply too few good advocates: too
many are attempting things that are over their heads. Judges
are heard increasingly to complain about inadequate performances. Some of the performances are outrageously bad, and this
is a matter of deep concern. Every judge has felt the almost
irresistible pressure and mesmeric power of a great advocate.
Many who appear before us are true advocates: they advance
the cause they serve with skill, confidence and expedition.
They do not need advice from us or from anyone else. Their
problem is not how to be an effective advocate; it is how to
cope with the storm of business that success brings — everyone

wants them. Sir Patrick Hastings, a great British barrister, put it this way:

> In every profession there is clearly defined, as though traced upon a map, the moment when the period of real anxiety has passed. It is easy to describe. For a long time the young professional, be he barrister or doctor or, indeed, engaged in any other walk of life, wants everything; he wants money, he wants work, he wants clients, and nobody in the world wants him. And then for no apparent reason everything is changed. Clients begin to want him; they seek his services; they consider themselves fortunate if he is on their side. He has reached the point when he is not merely wanting but has become one of the wanted. Then he has passed the Rubicon. With ordinary good fortune his career has become established and he will not look back.[1]

At the other end of the scale from the true advocates are a few unfortunate souls who are simply fish out of water. Their floundering and gasping for breath are pitiful to behold. Throw them life-lines as one will, they are beyond help. Sooner or later they disappear and are not seen again in court. That is just as well for them, in my opinion, for some I have seen do very well once they have found their niche outside the courts.

Between these extremes is a spectrum of competence, from mediocre through middling to good. The object of this book is to help those who hope to move up through the ranks. Most could if they tried.

Most beginners at the Bar have quick, bright minds, good intentions, youth and vigour, ambition and promise. For the most part they have worked hard: in law school, in their office, and on the case in hand. They are presentable, hopeful,

---

[1]*The Autobiography of Sir Patrick Hastings* (London, Wm. Heinemann Ltd., 1948), p. 143.

earnest, serious and courteous, but many are ineffective. Some can get through a case without calamity but many run close to it in the process. Some mumble and wander. Some conduct a little battle with themselves, raising points only to demolish them, losing their place, chasing papers, running around the court, huddling with witnesses, oblivious to all but the world they alone inhabit at the moment. Some read at length from law reports, to themselves. At last they sit down, some with surprising abruptness. Their case is not so much completed as exhausted. Whether the judge has understood them, or even heard them, does not seem to have crossed their minds.

Beginners who do these things are not necessarily bad lawyers but they have not yet learned the advocate's skills. At that stage they are easy meat for a capable opponent.

Sometimes both counsel are lacking in skill or experience. When they have finished the judge sadly contemplates the alternatives. He or she has had little help. What to do? Allow or dismiss the case then and there? Might that not be irresponsible? But does the judge's responsibility extend to doing counsel's job for them? Shall the case be added to the list of reserved judgments in the hope that in the future the time might be found to sit down and try to sort the thing out? A future filled with "reserves" is a terrifying prospect for a judge; that way lies madness. The temptation to abrupt disposition is very strong.

Beginners at the Bar are not the only offenders. The Bar divides into the good, the bad and the indifferent. I have often found myself wondering why it is that people who are obviously capable of doing a good job do a poor one. Presumably they are hoping to win. They have demonstrated sufficient capacity to learn that they have survived law school and the bar admission course. Yet they seem frustrated and irritable; the system seems to baffle them. They appear to think that the judge is trying to hinder them. In the result they have a miserable time in court and perform badly.

The answer to the question is simple although it may not be obvious. What separates the good from the bad at the Bar is, for the most part, training and experience. Since experience itself is training-ground, I may speak of both as training. Generally speaking, good counsel have been well trained, mediocre counsel badly trained and bad counsel untrained. There are many other factors that distort potential competence into incompetence: arrogance, ill-temper, petulance, lack of sympathy or empathy, lack of a plan or even of an understanding of the process are some. In my opinion all of these are secondary to lack of training and can be eradicated, or at least greatly ameliorated, by it. I think most judges would agree.

The difference in the extent and quality of training is astounding. It may be hard to believe, but it is true, that some lawyers walk into court *with no training at all*. I am not speaking of training in law schools or bar admission courses: I am speaking of training in court work. There is nothing wrong with law schools and bar admission courses. They are capable of training students of law to know and do many things, but they are not capable of teaching anyone to conduct a case in court. That requires training of a different kind, one that is these days pretty much a do-it-yourself affair. You must either be trained by others or train yourself. You may find neither method easy and both can be arduous, but without training you will get nowhere. Lack of training guarantees ineptitude: Every judge has his favourite story; the following are from my experience.

Before telling them I must give an explanation. I am conscious that some of the examples I use for illustration in this book might sound like pontification. Let me say at once that is not intended. The impulse to set these things down on paper stems from the many appalling gaffes that I myself committed through inexperience at the Bar. In some of the examples I use for illustration, I may not be the judge, I may be the lawyer. It is my hope that by revealing some of the gaucheries I have committed, or witnessed, I will save others from the embarrassment I suffered or watched. That impels me to set them down here, painful as they are to recall.

In a contract case plaintiff's counsel called his first witness. The evidence did not appear to be to his satisfaction. Attempts to improve it were met by objections from the other side. After a painful interval it dawned on the judge that counsel did not know what evidence the witness could give. An adjournment to chambers followed. The judge inquired why counsel was conducting an examination for discovery of his own witness. The young man revealed that this was his first time in court; in *any* court. He thought that he was not permitted to speak to a witness beforehand. Even his own witness! The judge adjourned long enough to allow him to speak to *all* his witnesses, or at least find out what they were going to say.

In another case — a domestic dispute — another young lawyer sought an adjournment on the ground that his client (the wife) had been taken to a hospital and could not appear when the case would be called the following day. He did not know which hospital nor what ailed his client. The judge informed him that he would need a letter from a medical doctor to support the request because respondent husband was pressing a counterclaim and desired to go on. The next day the young man turned up without his client and without a so-called "doctor's certificate" or even a line of writing from any doctor. He explained that he had been unable to get in touch with his client's doctor. At that point the husband's counsel rose to say that the wife had phoned his office during the previous week to say she did not wish to continue with the case. That was news to her counsel who, by this time, was thoroughly confused. The kindly judge offered a 15-minute break to allow the young man to sort things out. As the judge rose to leave, the young man said, "Would you do me a favour?" "What favour?", the judge asked, thinking, "What on earth is going on here?" "Would you phone the doctor?" said the young man. The judge narrowly avoided fainting and tottered out.

These things could not have happened without an almost total lack of training. Yet more than that is revealed. They disclose an assumption that training is not necessary. The ineptitude of counsel can lead to the loss of a case. That is not simply because counsel are inept: some cases succeed despite that. It is because through ineptitude they fail to prove a case. They don't know how to go about it. Their clients are victims of the naive belief on the part of their lawyers that any one can simply walk into court, "do what comes naturally", and have everything come out all right. Yet it would never have occurred to any such lawyer that he could graduate from law school without taking the course.

Granted the examples I have given are extreme. Yet they reveal what is almost every day demonstrated in court: that many lawyers appearing in the courts simply fail to grasp what it is all about. Judges are not looking for foible and error in counsel; they are looking for help. The quality of a trial, the quality of a decision, the quality of justice itself depends heavily upon the quality of counsel. Judges are always hoping for effectiveness, directness, candour and, above all, organization. All too frequently they are disappointed; the performance is inadequate. Their hearts sink. Frustration and anger might not be concealable. Another unhappy experience for everyone!

It is not easy to say why it is that people with sufficient ability to achieve a call to the Bar walk into court with no training at all. Perhaps the fault lies in our present system of legal education, which exists almost entirely separate from the actual practice of law and affords students little or no opportunity of experiencing life at the Bar. They may, as a result, simply lack a clear perception of the demands and difficulties of court practice. Could it be the consequence of watching the best counsel at work and inferring from their smooth and effortless performances that there is really nothing to it? Conversely, could it be the consequence of seeing the worst practitioners in action in the least demanding courts and imagining, as a result, that a low standard is acceptable?

Whatever the reason for having it, the idea that one can walk into court, without training, and hope for the best is a sure way to a rude shock. Successful advocates do not float in and out of court on a cloud. They put their brains, guts and lives into it and they keep doing that until the end. Nothing less will do.

The same things could be said about anyone who practises a difficult and demanding profession. I doubt if the successful practice of surgery could justly be described in other terms.

It is possible that those who walk into court with little or no training are victims of the three great myths about advocacy: "Advocacy is an art"; "Advocates are born, not made", and

"Advocacy cannot be taught". Belief in these is widespread. It is also pernicious. It puts competence as an advocate beyond the reach of the believer and keeps down many who have the capacity to rise. Let us look more closely at these chestnuts.

.

CHAPTER 3

THE THREE GREAT MYTHS

WE HEAR THE slogans "Advocacy is an art", "Advocates are born, not made" and "Advocacy cannot be taught" on every side. They were current when I was in law school and they are current today. Everyone seems to believe them. No bar association dinner is complete without another candle being lit on the altar of advocacy as art. Breath-holding accounts of the exploits of great advocates (some written by themselves) maintain the impression that such skills must be God-given and polish the image of the advocate as artist.

If these myths were simply harmless we could all afford to ignore them, but they are not harmless. They dissuade beginners who, unable to descry any God-given gift for advocacy among their skills, give up before they start. They discourage those who have had the courage to try their hand from trying to improve. The result is that we are left with a shortage of really first-rate advocates. There is, of course, nothing new in that. There have always been, and perhaps will always be, too few at the top. If such myths as these are contributing to that situation there is cause for attempting to eradicate them.

The truth can be expressed just as succinctly: "Advocacy is a skill that can be an art"; "Advocates are not so much born as made"; and "Even if advocacy cannot be taught it can be learned". I believe that I can prove all of these, but first I think it is worthwhile trying to find out how the myths arose.

The idea that advocates are born, not made, comes easily to mind when one is watching great advocates at work. The confidence they all exude, and the easy, graceful and brilliant performance of many make it all look so easy and natural that the onlooker thinks they must have been born to it.

They might think the same of a great pianist or ballet-dancer. Yet everyone has heard of the efforts pianists and dancers make to reach the top. The killing practice schedule, the search for great teachers, the ruthless exposure to competition; if there was anything God-given it was the will to succeed. Yet no one has ever heard of students of advocacy practising eight hours a day or moving from city to city to learn from great teachers. Does this not all mean that advocates are a breed apart, born into the world with a silver tongue in their little mouths, just waiting to grow up and stride into court?

In a word, No. Advocates must learn advocacy in order to succeed, just as ballet-dancers must learn dancing, and surgeons, surgery. Until a few years ago it was commonly said that "advocacy cannot be taught". Some law schools have bravely taken up the task, but it is too early to say how generally effective their efforts will be. Anyone who has ever attempted to teach advocacy must wish them well.

Asking, however, whether advocacy can or cannot be taught is asking the wrong question. The question is can it be learned? The answer is, Yes, it can be learned. As we shall see in the next chapter, there have always been ways of learning it, but basically advocacy is a self-taught skill. From the days of the Inns of Court would-be advocates have learned by assisting established advocates and watching them work and then trying out under supervision what they have learned.

This traditional process has produced many advocates whose God-given talents gave little promise of future success. Some, a fortunate few, have both innate talent and the desire to learn and with that combination are going inevitably to rise to the top. But there are many examples of successful counsel who, far from having any apparent innate talent, appeared to have been born with characteristics that would militate against any success at all. It is to these I turn for proof that you do not have to be born to be an advocate in order to succeed as one. They also demonstrate the fallacy of thinking that advocacy is an art and nothing else.

Professions may be no more than the most difficult crafts. Their practice demands a high level of dedication, responsibility and skill. Many a skill practised at its highest level is an art; there are cooks, skaters and actors who are so elevated by the quality of their work that they are artists, yet most who follow those callings do so at a lower but still respectable level. Law is no different and advocacy is no different. At the top there are a few artists. They have not achieved that status without unusual dedication and effort, whatever the quality of their original equipment.

I know that it does not look like that, and that no one wants to believe that it is so. I can hear you say, "It is all very well to hold up these shining examples, but surely these were people who were merely burnishing native talent?" Allow me to suggest that you look again. Some of the greatest achievers have succeeded not because they were born with great talent but despite being born with great deficiencies. We all have heard of great athletes who were born runtish or deformed. But do you know that one of the greatest advocates Canada has ever seen was born with a severe stammer? The late Walter Williston entered law school with the object of becoming a solicitor. With his speech defect it never occurred to him to attempt to be a court lawyer. Just before his call to the Bar an unpleasant personal experience created in him an iron determination to become a barrister. Through sheer grit, and the most painful imposition of self-discipline, he managed to reduce his speech defect to the point where he was able to present a case in court. Ultimately he reached the top, and achieved a national reputation, but he never wholly lost his stammer and never achieved easy eloquence. Yet, in a very short time after his call, he won a reputation as a coming man and, as everyone knows, went on to become one of the greats. If he had suggested to anyone before he made his decision to go to the Bar that he intended to practise as an advocate they might well have laughed at him.

He is but one example. There is more than one leading counsel in this country at the present time who is a stammerer.

The true mischief in the myth that advocates are born, not made, is not merely that it is untrue but that the reverse is frequently true. Many good and some great advocates have been made out of unpromising materials. You need but look around to see that a successful advocate may have been born with almost no talent for advocacy, or worse, with features of physique or personality that you might think would guarantee failure. Yet the capacity for the passionate pursuit of success that the best advocates must have overcame those obstacles and lifted them to the top.

For the good of the Bar, and of us all, I hope that these insidious myths may be swept away. They must be replaced with a general conviction that successful advocacy can be learned by almost anybody who wants badly enough to learn it.

CHAPTER 4

HOW TO LEARN ADVOCACY

I HAVE OBSERVED that advocacy has always been a largely self-taught skill. The traditional way to the Bar lay through a period of assistantship to an established advocate as student or junior. Through day-to-day association the learner saw how cases were prepared and presented. He or she sat in with counsel while instructing solicitors and witnesses were inter-viewed; carried bags and books to and from court and sat through trials taking notes and running errands, but above all watching and listening. After a time the fledgling was given a chance to try his wings in small matters in small courts. Larger responsibilities followed if that was done properly. In this orderly step-by-step fashion one found one's way to the Bar and to personal acceptance of the whole responsibility for the conduct of cases. The process was greatly facilitated by the articling system and the part-time law school. In my student days, from 1946 to 1949, and my early days at the Bar, I never heard of anyone who desired to learn advocacy being unable to find a place as student or junior with an established advocate or a firm where advocacy was practised.

Things have changed. I hear repeatedly from young lawyers how difficult it is to find a place where the kind of experience I have described may be obtained. It is difficult to say what has been most responsible for this change, but the enormous increase in the number of law students must be a big factor.

18

The system has not accommodated well to this crush of numbers, at least so far as learning advocacy is concerned.

No one wishes for a return to part-time law schools and there have been some notable attempts by law school faculties to fill the gap, but the fading of the traditional path to the Bar has begun to show some unfortunate consequences that seem to be increasingly noticeable in the courts. Stop-gap measures have not been generally effective. Bar associations and law societies hold seminars on advocacy and they are well attended and well conducted, but they are an inadequate substitute for the system we have virtually lost. It may be that another system will be found, better than the old and open to all. Whether the period of change we are in becomes a period of transition to a new era in which advocacy is taught on a disciplined and organized basis by law schools or in bar admission courses remains to be seen. For the present, for those who cannot wait for the millenium it is catch-as-catch-can and every one on his own. You are a student in search of a school; a pupil in search of a teacher.

How does one go about it? Some of the large firms continue, as before, to train their own advocates, but not all do and only a fraction of the great number called yearly to the Bar can hope to take advantage of that opportunity. Most set up on their own or find a place in a small firm which is not likely to have a litigation department. For the would-be advocate in that situation self-education is not a luxury, it is crucial.

You must, therefore, try to get all the instruction you can where you can; but you must seek it out, it will not seek you out. So you must go to the seminars, week-end courses and the like. There are some good books: read them. They can help, but you cannot learn to be an advocate simply by reading books any more than you can learn how to swim or fly-cast for trout. Sir Patrick Hastings put it aptly:[1]

> During my first two years I think I tumbled into nearly all the pitfalls, but each was a valuable experience because it taught me the best way to clamber out, and there is no other way of learning. Advocacy cannot be learned by reading law books any more than a boxer can learn to fight by merely punching at a ball. He has got to be knocked down many times before he is fit to earn his living in the ring.

He means, of course, "merely" by reading law books. You have only to read his autobiography to know the lengths to which he went, including, no doubt, reading everything on the subject, to train himself for the Bar.

A point to watch about books: be a little wary of those written for jurisdictions other than your own. The practice of advocacy is universal but the details may differ from one locale to another. It is possible that the hapless young man I mentioned in Chapter 2, who believed that witnesses could not be interviewed before they were called to the witness box, got the idea from books written for English barristers. The English rule does prevent barristers from interviewing witnesses privately, but permits it in the presence of instructing solicitors. Perhaps the young man in my example missed that refinement.

When you are in court waiting for your case to come on, watch and listen. Do not worry that you are not always watching the best examples. You can learn something of "how to do it" by watching good advocates but you can also learn how not to do it by watching poor ones.

I hope this is not beginning to sound like "listen to how I became a great counsel". I make no claim to a place in the

---

[1] *Op. cit.*, p. 92.

Pantheon of great Canadian counsel, and it is for that very reason that I believe I am qualified to speak, for I think that I made all the mistakes there were to make and have therefore a keen sympathy with those whom I see repeating the same old mistakes in the courts in which I sit. I have a sneaking suspicion that the real greats do not always have much understanding of what the rest of us go through, never having gone through it themselves, or, having done so, have forgotten it after reaching the top.

What I did manage to learn of advocacy was gained through close and constant association with two outstanding advocates over a period of five or six years. In addition, I had the great fortune to attend in what is now motions court in Toronto every day it sat for about a year. The matters I appeared on were minor, and because of that, and the judges' habit of calling on Queen's Counsel first, I was usually a long way down the list. The result was that I watched almost everyone practising at the Toronto Bar perform. I was astonished at the variance in performance. Even a know-all like myself could hardly avoid learning something once he realized he had something to learn. Dull old motions court became an exciting experience. I had a free and permanent seat at the play, and every day the bill and the players changed. I was sorry to leave when forced to move on to bigger things.

That is why, when I am presiding in motions court, I have a strong urge to say to people awaiting their turn, "Don't go out and stand gabbing in the hall, stay here and watch! This is and profit from it. Here is a place to learn what to do and what not to do at no cost or embarrassment to yourselves but a school of advocacy, as well as being a court; seize the chance simply by watching others."

I do not say it, of course; I do not have the courage. That is why I have chosen this means to try to get my message across — that if you would learn advocacy you must teach yourself, and that the only true advocacy academy is the court.

CHAPTER 5

THE ADVOCATE'S TASK

ONE THING THAT sets the adversary system of trial apart from others is that the judge's role is intended to be passive. Judges are not investigators; they are watchers and listeners. Counsel have the active role; they "present" the case. If the presentation is deficient it is not the judge's fault. If a witness is not called or an argument not made the error is not for the judge to rectify, however hard the self-restraint might be. The judge may intervene in order to clarify a point or resolve his or her or the jury's confusion but must not assume, or even appear to assume, an advocate's role. To do that would be to lose the neutrality of the judge and could be reversible error. In essence, the judge's task is to sit patiently, watch closely, listen carefully and decide justly.

That is the principle. It is not always followed in practice. There are legitimate ways for a judge to intervene. In Chapter 15 I will speak of illegitimate ways in which judges sometimes intervene and how to deal with them. My object here is to draw attention to the fact that the responsibility for the presentation of a case, or a defence, rests not on the judge but on counsel.

In designing the presentation counsel's problem is how to put his or her best foot forward. Every case has strong points and weak points. However strong a case may appear counsel cannot simply walk in and dump it on the court room floor. Cases so strong that they cannot be defended, or so weak that they cannot succeed, are not likely to go to trial. They will probably be settled or abandoned. The case that goes to court has become a conundrum with two answers. There are two sides with competing views. Every case has weaknesses and the weaknesses become more apparent as the pre-trial process of investigation and discovery proceeds. No one can count on "absolute truth" shining through: it is a concept unknown to the law. There are few "open and shut" cases. The outcome of a case turns on inference, probability, likelihood, interpretation. The evidence, however strong it appears, can be made through cross-examination to look equivocal. In spite of its appearance to laymen as a defined, even rigid, structure "the law" is equivocal: it must be "interpreted". Choosing one interpretation involves rejecting another. The trial process is an attempt by two contestants with differing views to persuade a judge that they are right. It is a complex, difficult, sensitive and risky affair. The decision will inevitably be highly subjective.

The decision in a case depends on how it looks to the particular court at the particular time. A trial judge may see it one way, but the subjectivity inherent in the process may be revealed by an appeal court seeing it differently and reversing the trial judgment. They are both looking at the same picture but they may see it differently. Two judges on a court may see a case in one way. A third sees it differently and dissents. Again they are all looking at the same picture, they have read the same material and heard the same arguments.

What could be more subjective than the concepts of fairness and natural justice? A court of three judges sees the resignation of a police officer after an all-night session of interrogation by superiors as forced and unfair; another court of three judges sees no unfairness. What is a proper sentence? What is a fair and adequate award of damages for an injury? Was there fraud or merely mistake? Has the onus been met? Such questions lie at the heart of the process. They are not peripheral. The answers involve a high degree of subjectivity, and for that reason are subject to the persuasive influence of counsel.

This was most vividly revealed to me when I began sitting in the Divisional Court, a court of three. I was struck by the frequency with which we would all think, after hearing an appellant (or applicant), that his case appeared unanswerable but, after hearing the respondent, would wonder how we could have thought there was anything in it. Such is the power of advocacy. I repeat that story here because I have told it many times to lawyers interested in the Divisional Court, and I have found even seasoned counsel to be surprised by it. The experience is not, of course, confined to that court. It was merely more vivid there.

Counsel must believe, and believe wholeheartedly, in the power of advocacy. Counsel's task is thus to paint a picture that the court will buy. It is to use the best colours in a limited palette; to avoid off colours and bad images. It is a complex, difficult and demanding job. All too often it is not done well simply because counsel do not realize how subjective the process is, and how susceptible it is to the skill of the advocate. The practice of advocacy is the practice of persuasion and the task is not finished until the trial is complete, for no case is lost before judgment has been given. Do not, as many do, give up half-way through. Stay with it: fight to the end. Like the last ticket drawn in the lottery, your last point might be the winner. Remember, "it's never over till it's over".

CHAPTER 6

ADVOCACY IS PERSUASION

THE LATE GREAT Joe Sedgwick used to tell us, "You catch more flies with honey than you do with vinegar". It is surprising how many lawyers do not understand that simple homily. Some seem to think that advocacy is simply "winning through intimidation", the theme of recent books on how to succeed in business. They discover that judges are, as a group, hard to push around. Some lawyers come into court for the first time with a mystifying air of contempt. Do they get this from watching television or movies? The source is immaterial. The attitude is entirely self-defeating. Others appear to think that the judge will do their job for them. They simply throw the problem at the judge, throw up their hands and walk out. These attitudes are not typical, but judges see them repeatedly. They are wholly at odds with the object of a court appearance, which is to persuade the court that what you propose is what should be done.

Counsel work is salesmanship; salesmanship of a high order, if you like, but salesmanship nonetheless. The late Douglas Laidlaw was a counsel of immense skill. He attributed much of his success to his student days as a perambulating purveyor of belts, braces, garters and arm-bands. (For younger readers I should explain that braces are suspenders for trousers, that arm-bands kept one's shirt cuffs at a desirable level, and that gentlemen wore garters to hold up their socks.) One thing a salesman learns is that no one of elementary intelligence would imagine he could sell a button by flinging it angrily across the counter at the customer. Similarly, the justice of a cause cannot be "sold" by such methods. Anyone wondering about his or her lack of success, or even lack of satisfaction in court, might consider coming down to earth and watching a good salesman sell.

Some would-be counsel have a fixed idea that judges *must* do what "the law requires". They appear to believe that the ineptitude, belligerence or offensiveness of counsel are irrelevancies that judges are duty-bound to ignore. That is a purely mechanical view of the process: the judge is a machine; one puts in a nickel, the machine clicks and whirrs and out pops the answer. Why, then, is it not the answer counsel demanded? Perhaps because the mechanical mind capable of holding such a view was incapable of recognizing the human factors that were important in the case. Judges must strive for justice and must try to ignore the failings of counsel; that is true. But the mechanical view puts counsel at a disadvantage for two reasons. One is the insensitivity to the human factors in the case; I have mentioned that. The other is that judges are human and might not be able to set aside entirely the behaviour of counsel. It is necessary to state that judges are human notwithstanding the sound of hollow laughter from those who have found that the tempers of some judges are nasty, brutish and short. Yet that is the very thing that proves the point. Being raised above the scuffle in the well of the court does not make them into gods. They remain mortally sensitive to offensive conduct and, like other mortals, are stung by insult or contempt or anger and react against it.

Offensive action should be expected, in court or out, to

generate an equal reaction. It might show immediately in a rude or ill-tempered response. That is bad enough, but the other consequences, and the subconscious effect, may be worse. How that can occur has never been better described than by Francis L. Wellman in his famous *The Art of Cross-Examination.*[1] In speaking of the necessity for proper demeanour in court, he said:[2]

> The counsel who has a pleasant personality; who speaks with apparent frankness; who appears to be an earnest searcher after truth; who is courteous to those who testify against him; who avoids delaying constantly the progress of the trial by innumerable objections and exceptions to perhaps incompetent but harmless evidence; who seems to know what he is about and sits down when he has accomplished it, exhibiting a spirit of fair play on all occasions — he it is who creates an atmosphere in favour of the side which he represents, a powerful though subconscious influence with the jury in arriving at their verdict. Even if, owing to the weight of testimony, the verdict is against him, yet the amount will be far less than the client has schooled himself to expect.
>
> On the other hand, the lawyer who wearies the court and the jury with endless and pointless cross-examinations; who is constantly losing his temper and showing his teeth to the witnesses; who wears a sour, anxious expression; who possesses a monotonous, rasping, penetrating voice; who presents a slovenly, unkempt personal appearance; who is prone to take unfair advantage of witness or counsel, and seems determined to win at all hazards — soon prejudices a jury against himself and the client he represents, entirely irrespective of the sworn testimony in the case.

He was speaking there of appearing before a jury, but only a hypocrite would claim that judges are not similarly affected.

That is not to say that you must be unctuous. Trials, as indicated in the next chapter, are not tea parties, and most

---

[1] 4th ed. (N.Y., Macmillan, 1962).
[2] Page 34.

judges have participated in many trials before going to the Bench. It follows that both judges and counsel become a little case-hardened and accustomed to more strenuous give and take than would be acceptable outside court. Most judges are not, therefore, looking for excessive politeness from counsel: straight talk will do. The level of straight talk that is routine to judges and experienced counsel can appear as rudeness to a layman. Not long ago there was an appeal in the Supreme Court of Canada that not even the most sanguine on the appellant's side thought would be easy. The task was to overturn a decision of the Ontario Court of Appeal on contingent remainders written, without a dissent, by the unchallenged expert on the subject, Bora Laskin, J.A. The sister of appellant's counsel attended as a spectator. Brother and sister had arranged lunch, for the appeal was to come on in the morning and was not expected to take long. It did not. The other side was not called on. Shortly after appellant's case was opened, the court began asking some rather searching questions. Counsel did with them what he could. Looking around, he found his sister had left. The court adjourned for lunch. He went to where lunch had been arranged and found his sister in a distressed state. She had never before been in a court. She had left because she couldn't stand hearing her brother treated that way. "Who was that rude old man at the end who would never let you finish a sentence?" she asked, naming a distinguished judge, now retired. Brother was astonished. He thought, and said, that he had had a pretty good hearing, considering the difficulty of the case. He had not expected an easy ride. She did not see it that way; to her it looked like a bear pit.

So the level of courtesy required at the Bar has nothing to do with the kind of directness, even abruptness, that would not do in ordinary social intercourse. You may be as forthright as you please and no one will complain.

You may go further than that: you may be rigorous, sharp, aggressive and pointed; even harsh, as the occasion requires. But you may never be devious, unfair, rude, ill-tempered, contemptuous, "personal" or dishonest. You must never abuse a witness. Above all, you must never mis-state the evidence or mislead the court in any way. That is beyond the limit. Do any such thing and you will regret it. You might avoid a scalding reaction but you might wonder why, in future cases before other judges, you are treated as though you are something just beyond the reach of a ten-foot pole, or never invited into their chambers for a friendly chat.

Long exposure might have hardened some judges to the kind of conduct that laymen would react strongly against, but do not depend upon it. Everyone has a breaking point, or a bad day when his or her resistance is low. Only a fool would deliberately set out to test the limits of a judge's patience or capacity to endure ineptitude or offensiveness. Keep in mind that judges are human. It is even more important to remember that, in a slightly altered version of Shylock's famous cry, when you scratch them, you bleed.

CHAPTER 7

A TRIAL IS NOT A TEA PARTY: WHAT THIS MEANS TO COUNSEL

"...A JURY TRIAL is a fight and not an afternoon tea."[1] Nor is it a high school debate, a beauty contest, a dogfight or a war. Most judges have watched trials that resembled one or the other of all of these. The counsel who conducted them had in every case missed the point.

Some cases win themselves despite the shortcomings of counsel. For the most part, however, a trial is a duel. It is a battle of wits: a test of intellectual strength, skill and will in which counsel are the protagonists. For the parties the stakes can be high: life imprisonment in one case, impoverishment in another. The winner is likely to be the side with the greater strength, the greater skill and the greater will to win. For counsel, winning and losing is less crucial (see Chapter 16). What *is* crucial is their performance. How did they appear? Did they create an impression as masters of their craft or as inept bumblers?

Whether a case appears to be a "winner" or a "loser" is of small significance to top counsel. They accept that they will be retained sometimes because the case appears to be a loser. Tough cases test their mettle. They go into court determined to win, and the weaker the case the greater the test.

---

[1]Riddell J.A., in *Dale v. Toronto R.W. Co.* (1915), 34 O.L.R. 104 at p. 108, 24 D.L.R. 413 at p. 416.

The mental set required for the task is the vision of oneself as the protagonist: the champion chosen to fight for the better side. Nothing less will do.

The strain of a trial can be intense. To be successful, or even to survive without breaking down, counsel must learn to rely on themselves completely. They must, as was said of Winston Churchill, "give full credence to their own opinions". Decision after decision must be made at trial, many on the spur of the moment. Counsel must decide, without more than a moment to reflect, whether to cross-examine or to refrain, to call or not to call a witness, to object or to sit still, any one of which decisions may be of critical importance. Counsel must decide whether to try to settle or to fight on, whether to change or maintain the strategy initially adopted, and, while they would be foolish not to consult those around them, their juniors and other assistants, they are always keenly aware that they must bear on their own shoulders the full responsibility for the decision.

All of this conspires to create in successful counsel an unshakeable confidence in their own abilities. To others, that may appear to be simple egotism. If egotism implies preferring your own opinion to that of others, then I think it may fairly be said that, while not all of them will admit it, top advocates tend to have big egos. That might not be news; so do top surgeons, top actors, top anything. The point is that they believe they are better than the other side and do their best in every case to prove it. They never let up. They hate to lose. They are always studying their craft, learning from others, testing new techniques, measuring their adversaries, pushing themselves harder. Their life is exacting and exhausting. Some crack up. Many give up temporarily but come back to it.

Some feel burnt out by fifty, or even earlier, and look forward to the prospect of what appears to them to be an easier life on the Bench.

There is a lot to be said against that kind of life. It is hard on health, mental balance and domestic tranquillity. It is one-dimensional, obsessively concentrated on tackling the next case, and the next and the next. In the seventies it would have been classified and written off by the knowing as an "ego trip". It was said of Williston that "he didn't win cases, he beat people". The thrill of beating a tough adversary can be heady. One successful counsel once observed that counsel work could be his only possible vocation, because when he won he knew few others could have won, and when he lost he knew no one could have won.

The point of this is not whether as a lifestyle it would be endorsed by philosophers. The point is that when you enter the arena of the court room you are sooner or later going to face that kind of adversary. As the flood of new lawyers pours into the Bar the going is going to get rougher. You will have to be good to survive; to flourish, you will have to be very good.

You must remember this in every case: every time you rise in a court room you risk your case and your reputation. Crossing swords with a dedicated duellist in the court room can be very humbling; if your heart is not in it you should find some other line of endeavour. Not even a "good" case can always save you. A successful English barrister once commented upon how many good cases he lost when he was young and how many bad cases he won when he was old.

You have to do your best every time because you are being watched. The court room is an arena and you are one of the gladiators. Every time you stand up you have an audience.

You might think it is just the judge and jury, but that is not so. You are being watched by everyone in court: the court clerk, the constables, the ushers, the sheriff's deputy, the witnesses, your opponents, their counsel, sometimes a room crammed with spectators. They will all go out and talk about you. The reputation of a real trial counsel is made in court. That is where it can also be lost. In every case you are on display. Part way through a murder trial the constable in charge of the jury surprised me with a question from the jury. They wished to know defence counsel's name!

We all know of lawyers who appear to make their living in court but whose court room performances are less than adequate. It is possible to make a living in court and yet be a very bad counsel. The explanation is rarely far to seek.

Some have married the boss's daughter. They have "connections" — family or business ties that produce court work for them whether they deserve it or not. They are satisfied to take advantage of that situation and heedless of their standing in the eyes of their peers. One can only have sympathy for their clients and for the judges who must put up with them. The same situation must exist elsewhere. A knowledgeable author writing of the English Bar in 1960 estimated that half of the members of the practising Bar had some family relationship with a solicitor.

Some who are truly inept have simply persuaded their solicitor partners that they are good counsel, and because the solicitors never go to court, and do not know many (or any) judges or other counsel, they accept the self-appraisal. They might wonder about it, but solicitors are surprisingly quick to think that the whole court process is a mystery governed by its own rules and standards and to suspend their own judgment.

Other bad counsel are retained *because* they are bad, not in spite of it. Some people involved in litigation, and even some solicitors, engage counsel in the hope that they will confuse the enemy, frighten them with threatening gestures or delay the case until the other side becomes disheartened and gives up. Some counsel are engaged because they will do almost anything their clients ask them to do. That can include simply acting like a dog on a rope that will bark and growl at his master's command.

Not long ago there was at the Bar an elderly gentleman who was almost constantly in court. For that reason he was entitled to call himself "counsel". He might not have had many cases but he managed to squeeze out of every case a very considerable amount of employment. That was because in every case he launched a fusillade of motions and when the case finally got to trial and he lost, as he usually did, he immediately offered the other side the choice of settling or going through an appeal. It mattered not that there was not the smallest merit in the appeal. For him the merit lay in the fact that the appeal brought further expense and delay and appeal he did, up to the Supreme Court of Canada, in one case more than once.

That man was a real threat, indeed he was a menace, and those who found themselves on the side opposed to him were well advised to consider settling not because of any lack of confidence in their case or in their counsel but simply because that man took an undue advantage of the weaknesses of the system. In court he violated almost every precept that we lay down in this book. He was not alone. There were others like him. There are others like him in every generation of barristers. Do not be misled by such examples.

The mere fact that someone is related to a solicitor does not make him or her a bad counsel; there are too many examples that prove the contrary. But if you wonder why an inept counsel seems to enjoy regular employment a few inquiries will likely reveal the secret. Most would-be counsel are without a life-support system that will permit them to survive however inept they are. Most have to battle for success on their own and most prefer it that way. As my co-author says later, it keeps the adrenalin flowing.

CHAPTER 8

KNOW THE RULES

As MOST JUDGES will tell you, it is simply astonishing how many lawyers who appear in court do not know the Rules of Court. You cannot hope to succeed, except in looking foolish, if you do not know the Rules. Do not depend on what someone in a court office told you. They are not paid to advise you, and if you know what you are about you will not ask them. You sound pretty feckless when you stand up in a crowded court and say, when asked by a sceptical judge on what authority you rest, "Miss J. in the court office told me." It is surprising how many times that happens. On the last occasion on which it happened in my court there must have been thirty lawyers present. When the poor fellow made that answer to my question, everyone tittered. He did not seem to notice, but if I had been in his place I think I might have died on the spot.

Anyone with the brains to get through law school can, with a little effort, learn the Rules and learn them well. The great racing driver Stirling Moss won some races simply because he knew the rules better than other drivers. He has sagely observed: "If you don't know the rules you shouldn't be in the race."

The advocate's skills must be learned from the ground up. Williston taught us that first you learn the Rules, then you learn the forms, then you learn "the law". Before that you have no business being in court. It matters not that you are stuffed with law; if you do not know the Rules you cannot use it.

If my experience is any guide, I would venture to say that every day in our courts there are causes damaged or lost, and counsel confounded, simply because they have failed to master the Rules.

This is a good point at which to add: learn also the rules of evidence. Judges are complaining more and more about counsel who appear to know little, or even nothing, about the law of evidence. While I was writing this chapter a fellow judge came fuming into the lunch room. He told us that, in the trial over which he was presiding, plaintiff's counsel had called a witness as an expert but had not sought to qualify him as such. The judge found himself in the predicament of having himself to question the witness to ascertain the state of his expertise, for counsel did not appear to know how to cope with that. When that was out of the way, counsel continued questioning his witness with the evident intention of eliciting the hearsay opinions of the witness's assistant. At that point the judge exploded. Who can blame him? Counsel are expected to know the law of evidence, at the very least to the extent of not deliberately seeking to offend the hearsay rule.

If you do not understand the rudimentary rules of evidence you will not be excused by judges on the ground that you "didn't take a course". If you have the hardihood to embark upon the trial of an action while remaining ignorant on the subject of evidence you not only run the risk of being scolded, or embarrassed; you leave yourself open, in my opinion, to a charge of professional irresponsibility, or even a suit for negligence. On that subject see the decision of Krever J. in

Demarco v. Ungaro et al.,[1] essential reading for all counsel.

As you can see from my retelling of the anecdote heard in the judges' lunch room, your reputation can be made by such conduct, but not in the way that most people would wish.

If you would climb the advocacy ladder, put your feet first on the bottom rung. Learn the Rules of Court and the rules of evidence.

---

[1](1979), 21 O.R. (2d) 673, 95 D.L.R. (3d) 385.

CHAPTER 9

COURT ROOM CHOREOGRAPHY

THIS CHAPTER IS about where and where not to stand in court. Too elementary? Not so. Not more than one in fifty lawyers appearing in our courts knows where to stand. That must be because only a few realize how important it is.

Let us start with the commonest example of how not to do it. This happens in nearly every case. A witness is in the witness box. Counsel wishes to introduce a document. Counsel walks up to the witness box and stops on the side away from the judge. The witness turns towards counsel. Now the judge has a view of the back of the witness's head; his or her view of counsel is blocked by the witness. Counsel then shows the witness the paper. They stand side by side reading it. "Have you seen this before? Is that your signature? I direct your attention to paragraph 2 . . .", etc.

This goes on. Counsel and the witness talk quietly to each other. They are having a little huddle. They talk quietly because they are so close to each other that it is unnecessary and would even be rude to raise their voices. But they have left the judge out. The judge cannot hear them and cannot even fall back on lip-reading, a device a judge sometimes resorts to in desperation, because their faces cannot be seen. The judge really wants to ask, "Do you mind if I overhear your conversation?", but is likely to settle for a mild "I cannot hear you".

If that does not produce results, he or she might put pen or pencil down and give up.

Why do counsel do this? Nothing is more irritating; nothing less effective in proving a case. I think they do it simply because they do not think about it. It goes without saying that no one ever told them how to do it correctly.

Once the error is pointed out it is easy to correct. Consciousness of that particular problem can lead counsel to an appreciation of the whole science of court room choreography. That is why it is worth pointing out.

To see the problem clearly let us look down from the dais. You see a traditional pattern. Before the judge sits the registrar or clerk; in front of him or her is the well of the court, then the counsel table. Beside the dais is the witness box (I am ignoring the jury for the moment). When counsel stands at the counsel table and questions a witness the witness turns towards counsel. The judge can see and hear counsel, and can see the witness's face in somewhat better than profile, observe the witness's expression and hear the answers. When counsel moves the witness's nose follows like a pointer. When counsel moves up to the side of the witness box away from the judge the nose points towards counsel and that other phenomenon of oral communication occurs: people lower their voices as they move closer together. By the time counsel reaches the witness box, both are mumbling. Another exercise in futility has begun.

The reason that counsel stands beside instead of in front of the witness is, of course, obvious. He or she wishes to point to the document being shown the witness and because most people cannot read a document upside down he or she must stand in the same viewing position as the witness.

If you can remember that a witness's nose homes on counsel like a compass needle on north, you can aim a witness in any direction you want. If you ask your questions from your place at the counsel table everyone will see the witness and hear his or her answer. When you know what you are about and have a document to introduce you offer the original and a copy to the registrar or clerk (or, if it is likely to be easier, hand the intended exhibit to the witness and a copy to the clerk for the judge). The clerk hands the original to the witness and a copy to the judge. You have copies for other counsel and hand them to them if you have not already done so. You stand at your place at the counsel table and say to the witness, "I show you a document. It appears to be a letter from you to X dated Do you recognize the document?", etc. The witness is reading the original document (or frequently, these days, a facsimile) that is to be offered as an exhibit. The judge is reading his or her copy. The other counsel sitting at the counsel table are reading their copies. There are no interruptions from other counsel, such as "I wonder if my friend will let me see that document? I don't remember it being produced on discovery," etc. There is no unseemly pile-up around the witness box as opposing counsel try to stay abreast of what is going on. I have seen opposing counsel actually climb up the back of the box in an attempt to see what was going on. I have actually watched a Q.C., who was questioning a witness in chief about a document, step up into the box with the witness and begin a little conversation in whispers.

When you do it correctly the witness's nose is pointed obliquely across the judge's dais. Because you have not moved closer to the witness you do not drop your voice; nor does the witness. Everyone can see; everyone can hear. When the document has been identified you ask that the document be marked as an exhibit and describe it briefly for the record. The clerk obtains the document from the witness and hands it to the judge. The judge examines it to ensure that it is legible and otherwise acceptable and, if it is acceptable, instructs the clerk to mark it as an exhibit. Into the record it goes as smooth as silk.

All of the following applies to jury trials as well. The pointer principle applies. Judges instruct juries to watch witnesses closely, but they cannot do so if counsel stand in the way. It is less important that the judge see and hear the witness because the jurors are the fact finders, but it is desirable that both can do so with ease. Do not huddle with the witness and exclude the jury, or stand between the witness and the jury, if you want the jury to receive the full impact of your evidence. By the way, the jury will not tell you if they cannot hear. In spite of the fact that judges always say in their opening instructions to juries, "If you cannot hear let me know", juries hardly ever speak up. In our combined seventy years at the Bar and on the Bench my co-author and I have experienced only a few occasions when jurors said they could not hear. Jurors appear to think that if you wish them to hear you will make sure they do. So have your witness's nose pointed in a direction that permits both judge and jury to see and hear. Again, directly towards the counsel table will do that nicely.

Defence counsel might prefer in jury trials to place a lectern at the far end of the jury box and conduct their examinations from there, for in some court rooms that might position them closer to the witness than they would be if they stood at their place at the counsel table.

It goes without saying that standing beside the witness for a mumbling session is even worse in a jury trial, because it is not only the judge who will not hear; it is the jury as well, and none of them will forgive you.

In appeal courts, and motions courts, you do not have to worry about witnesses; you have to make sure only that you are heard. I speak of the necessity for an audible voice at greater length in Chapter 14, but audibility and persuasiveness are affected as well by where you stand. "Front and centre" is the rule. Firing weakly from the back right upper corner of the court room is not going to improve your effectiveness. It is amazing how many lawyers will stand at the back of an empty court room, be asked repeatedly to speak up and never grasp the simple fact that if they moved up to the front and centre their problem would be cured and their effectiveness increased 100 per cent. Standing in the back corner of an empty court room makes you look as if you are preparing to run through the door if the judge asks you a question. That is bad for your credibility and effectiveness.

Squash players crowd the "T", the point on the floor where the service line intersects the division between right and left courts. It is the strategic point, the point from which the most effective play can be started. One can run up, run back and run sideways. Front and centre is the "T" of the court room. Squash players try to occupy and hold the "T". They try to keep opponents away from it and only polite mayhem is permitted. You do not have to worry about that in court. No one is trying to push you out of the "T". They cannot, for only one player is allowed to perform at a time. When your turn comes you can stride up, have the constable bring you a lectern if one is not already there, place it front and centre, take a deep breath and begin. Better still, ensure beforehand that a lectern is in the court room and placed where you wish it to be.

Remember also to stand still. Do not walk around; it is disturbing. While it has not yet happened to me a colleague has told me about counsel in his court who repeatedly asked questions of a witness while standing with his back to the witness, the judge and the jury! Had I not had similar experiences I might have found that difficult to understand. Some of these things must be seen to be believed.

If you do not use the court room to your advantage it will not be your opponents' fault; it will be yours. There is nothing they can do to stop you. They can only laugh at your ineptitude, and they will!

CHAPTER 10

HOW TO TELL THE PROS FROM THE DABBLERS

Court manners

MANNERS COUNT in court. A journalist, reporting the Supreme Court of Canada's hearing on the validity of proposed amendments to the Constitution, thought it sufficiently newsworthy to say:

> The Supreme Court is a different world. There is no room for rhetoric ... wit is elegant and restrained and rare. Manners are almost as studied as words.[1]

Studied manners offend some people, and we have with us graduates of an entire generation to whom good manners were decried as an elitist put-down. But before writing off the subject of good court manners as phony, unnecessary and out of date, consider this ringing truth: good court manners are the very mark of the best counsel.

There are exceptions. Some good counsel have borderline manners, and some who are usually well-mannered suffer lapses. But, by and large, in over thirty-eight years of observing counsel as a law student, lawyer and judge I think the rule is true. If it is not true at least the corollary is: bad manners are the mark of bad counsel.

Well, you might say, "Why should I bother with such stuff?

[1] *The Globe and Mail*, May 2, 1981, p. 13.

My manners are up to any reasonable standard. I do what mother told me, so let's skip to the next chapter." There is a little problem with that which I will try to illustrate.

Some customs and traditions

Good court manners are indeed usually nothing more than what is called "common courtesy". There are, however, many situations that arise when even courteous people might not know quite what to do. These situations are usually governed by custom or tradition. It might, for instance, be difficult to see anything discourteous about simply picking up your books and walking out of court when your case is over, even if it is the last case on the list for that day. Yet to do so could mark you as an ignoramus, be viewed as a discourtesy by other counsel and draw a tart rebuke from the judge. The reason for this is that even this simple situation is governed by immemorial custom, and if you do not adhere to the custom you could be in trouble. The governing rule is simple: you must not leave until you are excused. That applies whether you are the first case on the list or the last. If you are the last, you must wait either until you are excused or until after the judge "rises", which means leaves the court.

Now that might sound like a return to grade school, but when you think about it there are some good, if not obvious, reasons for this. In most courts, the last thing that a judge does with a case is to make a written endorsement on the record which he or she then reads aloud. That becomes the official disposition of the case. It will be copied by the clerk or registrar into the court register, and is the basis on which the formal judgment or order later issued must rest. So it is important to get it right. Any corrections or additions may, and should, be made right then and there. Counsel are expected to speak up if the endorsement is not satisfactory. That final precaution cannot be taken if counsel leave before they hear it read.

When I was at the Bar there was a judge who used to administer a little lesson to counsel who picked up and left before he had endorsed the record and read it out. He would use the endorsement to administer a little "shock treatment". Thus, he might write, "Appeal dismissed with costs" when he had, in fact, decided the reverse. When the successful counsel tried to take out the order he had quite a time. I do not know of any judge who does that in these kindlier times, and the tale is not told as a warning but as an illustration of the importance of custom and the possible consequences of ignoring it.

The customary dismissal is simply a "thank you" from the judge to counsel or even a nod in their direction. If you do not hear that, or words or a gesture to that effect, wait until the next case is called. Then you know your case is over and you may leave.

I do not know whether all the customs of the court can be traced back to some rational base, and I am not surprised about that because I am talking about customs that have existed for centuries. My point is that even if they do not appear to make a lot of sense they are there, and flouting them could make you look like a tyro. Another example of a perhaps obscure custom that does not appear to have anything to do with good manners relates to the telephone. Members of the Bar never telephone judges' chambers. I can think of nothing discourteous in it but it is never done. If you wish to get in touch with a judge you call his or her secretary.

I accept that some of these customs are hard to explain or justify and you are, of course, entitled deliberately to reject them. That is up to you. For example, some people have a strong distaste for bowing, which is dealt with later in this chapter. They will "bow their head to no man". That makes it difficult for them to observe the quaint tradition of judge and counsel bowing to each other in court. You may deliberately decide not to bow, claiming respect for your decision on the ground that bowing is demeaning and your rejection of it is the only acceptable practice for an egalitarian society. The trouble with that is that it will not appear that way; it will appear as if either you do not know any better or you are being deliberately discourteous. You can hardly hold up a sign saying "I am not bowing because that is elitist claptrap and I am an intelligent person". So no one will give you the credit you deserve.

Worse, you may well shake the confidence that others have in your judgment. The capacity to inspire confidence is crucial. You would not willingly impair that quintessential quality without which no true success as counsel can ever be gained.

The safer course is to learn the customs and traditions of the court, conform to them as much as your conscience permits and save your reforming zeal for something else.

I will shortly set out some examples of what I have been discussing. Before doing that, let me try to sum up the point of this chapter. As in any field of activity, there is a difference between the true professionals and the dabblers. It is instantly apparent in court. Basically, the difference consists in this: professionals know how to act and dabblers do not. How to act is largely governed by tradition. Some people respect and enjoy tradition; they are proud to be part of something enduring and to show that they are. Others hate it; tradition robs them, they feel, of their individuality. They are "against tradition" and do not hesitate to show it. Still others simply do not know the traditions and bumble along, unwittingly making all the mistakes. You are not obliged to observe the customs of the court, but your failure to do so will likely do your reputation some harm. Better to learn how it is done and do it.

I hope I do not sound unsympathetic to the anti-traditionalists, having been something of one myself. I hated saluting in my early days in the air force and came close to being placed on charge for it. Then I ran across another rugged individualist afflicted with a different foible: he refused to wear his cap. He thought caps were ridiculous. It was easier to avoid saluting than it was to avoid wearing your cap so my friend spent quite a few days behind bars paying for his obduracy. His example taught me two things: first, when you cannot win, give in; second, when standing up for your principles do not expect to get the credit you think you deserve. I did not like to tell him, but I thought refusing to wear a hat was ridiculous and going to jail for it was crazy. I had the queasy feeling that other people thought the same of me for refusing to salute.

The next little custom I am hesitant to mention because it seems so obvious; yet I have been surprised at how often it is ignored. When a judge is giving a ruling or a decision from the Bench it is inappropriate to talk, or to get up and wander about the court room. You would not do so if you were being addressed directly, but when someone else is involved some people take it as an opportunity to consult a client or witness sitting in the audience. The reason you should not do it is, of course, that it is distracting, not only to the judge but to counsel being addressed, as well as a discourtesy to others.

When you wish to speak or are addressed directly by the judge you must stand. Some years ago we had a well-known Crown attorney whose habit it was to speak, or growl, while seated at the counsel table. His long service at the Bar and his Irish wit had given him the status of a "character" in the magistrate's courts where he appeared, and, as such, he was allowed some eccentricities. Admiring young counsel who aped his habit of firing from the hip soon discovered that it was not tolerated from anyone else. Old Fred, the Crown attorney, was thought to have earned his "perk".

There are many stories of judges putting up with eccentricities in counsel's conduct. When they are traced back a little they are almost always found to involve counsel who have survived many years at the Bar. The law is a great respecter of age. Judges, who might have been their students, are loathe to admonish elderly counsel and, unless the eccentricity grows into offensiveness or to the point where it impedes the trial, tend to be tolerant. This sometimes seems unfair to young counsel, and perhaps it is, but it is there and it is likely to continue. Thus it was that on one occasion a young counsel was admonished from the Bench for wearing white socks in court, while in the same courts one could see the aristocratic face and figure of the aging "Mike" Chitty, Q.C., nationally known author and lawyer of great distinction and accomplishment, wearing his famous tattered silk gown, green with age, and walking about in his white sneakers.

The obvious principle is: do not try to get away with eccentric manners until you are too old and distinguished to be scolded. The corollary is, if you find you are getting away with things you should not be doing you might be older than you think!

To continue: when the judge is sitting gowned counsel must also be gowned. The judge "cannot see" ungowned lawyers, in the old phrase. The rationale for this is surely to ensure that the judge can tell at a glance whether the person addressing the court is a member of the Bar, and therefore gowned, or a member of the public acting for himself, and therefore not gowned. If you are ungowned and wish to address the court ask some gowned counsel to speak for you. By another tradition, counsel never refuse that request.

It is also traditional, when you are on your feet in court and must pause for longer than a moment or so to look for a paper or a citation, to say, "May I have a moment please?" It is also wise to observe this little nicety for by it you afford the judge an opportunity to inquire whether a moment will suffice and avoid the risk of having a judge say, "Mr. Blank, would you kindly get on with your case, we cannot wait all day," which looks bad on the record and before the jury. Above all, do not just stop in the middle of a sentence, mumble "court's indulgence" and then start digging around in your papers. You might see that on American television but it is not done here.

Counsel must never express their own opinion, as in, "I think the accused is not guilty". Their opinion is irrelevant. Indeed, they may believe the accused is guilty, yet strive, as they must, to win the case. If they offer an opinion to a judge, the judge might choose to grind teeth and remain silent; but if they express an opinion to a jury it will probably earn a rebuke, which is bad for counsel and bad for his or her case.

The best counsel do not say "Blue J." when they mean

Mr. Justice Blue. The "J." is a printer's device that means "Mr. Justice", or "Madam Justice". You would not say "White Co. Ct. J.", because you could not get your tongue around it. You would say "Judge White". Oh, I know, everyone says "Blue J." and the judges just sit there saying nothing. All that means is that they have given up trying to educate you. So go ahead and say it and prove you are second rate, or at least a mere dabbler.

Personal appearance

There are many other ways of proving that. I walk to court in the morning. Lawyers are hurrying to the court house, some with their clients and witnesses. I sometimes wonder what the clients think of them. There the clients are, on the way to a trial that means a lot to them, with a protagonist of their choosing who looks as if he has not had time to dress. Open-necked shirt, jeans and tabs, the wildest combination of court and street dress; a brief case in one hand and gown, waistcoat, collar, tabs and shirt all strung over the other arm and flying in the breeze. He looks as if, while shaving, he suddenly remembered he was in court that morning and already late.

Some, more particular about how they look, do not simply fling their gowns over their arm; they sling them over their shoulder in a zippered plastic bag embellished with the name of the clothing shop where they bought their last suit of clothes. Some favour air-line bags. The least fastidious, or the most hurried, it is hard to tell, actually carry their gown in a green plastic garbage bag. I say "actually" to mean I have witnessed that and know it to be true. I would not otherwise have believed it. Does a lawyer who is capable of carrying his gown to court in a green garbage bag have any idea what that says about him? Does he think that will inspire confidence in his professional ability in anyone but his mother?

Again, there are a few exceptions but the best counsel would never be seen in such a condition. They know and follow the tradition. While they might be seen in their gowns on the court house lawn taking the air during a break, they do not wear a mixture of street and court clothes on the street. They carry their gowns in the traditional blue (or red if a Q.C.) cloth bag. If you think you cannot afford a cloth bag there is nothing wrong with a brief case or travelling bag. But not a green garbage bag, not if you have any, even the slightest, regard for your reputation. Never!

Counsel would avoid many of these lapses if they kept it firmly in mind that they are officers of the court. In a literal sense the court cannot get along without them. This might be the basis for the tradition that requires counsel to ask leave to be excused from attending court in a case in which they have been engaged. An explanation is always offered — usually another court engagement — and leave is always given, but the custom of asking for leave serves to remind everyone that the court cannot function without counsel. The better counsel are the better it functions.

Punctuality

You should never be late, but some day you will be: fate will see to that. The first thing you must do when court opens is to apologize and explain the delay briefly. You need not cry or wring your hands. Be brief and sincere. Dabblers walk casually into court ten minutes late acting as if nothing were amiss. They look hurt and puzzled when the judge lands on them. Being pulled up for such a small thing is a bad way to start your case, or your day, particularly if it happens in front of your clients.

By the way, nearly all court clocks are wrong. The way to be on time is to set your watch by the court clock. Then you will never have to say, like a child in school, "My watch was slow". I once told a lawyer who excused his repeated tardiness on that ground that it was an excuse I did not permit my children. He was so cross that he appealed my decision in the case. (I know that was the reason because he later told me so.) That resulted in a waste of time and money for he had to find a better ground than that for his appeal and, failing to do so, lost the case a second time. I tell the story not to suggest that my decisions are unappealable but to illustrate how a little thing like being on time can affect the proceedings and, in particular, your composure.

Introducing other counsel

In courts where counsel slips are in use, when you rise to open a case introduce other counsel. Say, "May it please the court, I appear for the plaintiff; Ms. A. is with me; my friend Mr. X appears for the defendant Smith; Mr. B. is with him; my friend Mr. Y appears for the defendant Jones." Counsel being introduced stand when their name is spoken, bow and sit down.

You need not say, "My name is Fortiori, initial A", because you have filled out a counsel slip showing your name to be Albert (or A.) Fortiori before the trial opens and handed it to the court clerk or registrar. You have done this legibly and in such a fashion that the judge can tell by glancing at the slip who you are and for whom you appear. Counsel should not leave the task of filling out the counsel slip to the registrar for the very good reason that the registrar might get it wrong. Some registrars have no idea of the function of counsel slips. They will put down the names of law firms as counsel appearing, or out-of-town solicitors for whom some person — unnamed — is appearing. The function of a counsel slip is to tell the judge who is appearing and for whom. The object of standing to introduce yourself and others is to put names to faces. The judge is not interested in anything else, such as the names of firms or whose agent counsel is. It is astonishing what court registrars will write on counsel slips if it is left to them. Furthermore, some cannot write legibly. Another poor way to start a trial is to have a struggle over the counsel slips.

Women counsel must include the designation by which they wish to be addressed: Miss, Mrs. or Ms. That is essential but often overlooked. Many simply write down, for example, "Doris Doe". Do they really expect the judge to say, "Well, Doris, what is this case all about?"

A famous counsel, now a judge, used to mention another advantage of counsel slips. If your client is present in court he or she is unlikely to know about counsel slips. Thus, when the judge addresses you by name your client can hardly fail to be impressed.

In the lower courts, where counsel slips might not be used, learn the proper way to identify yourself and follow it. In such a court you will probably have to give your own name as well when introducing other counsel unless, of course, you are already known to the judge.

Ungowned assistants

If you wish to have ungowned assistants sit with you at the counsel table you should identify them and request leave to have them there. Leave, by tradition, is always given, but this device lets the judge know who is with you for their names will not appear on the counsel slip, and it underlines the status of counsel as officers of the court entitled to be present unless excluded by the presiding judge.

There is something else that should be said about ungowned assistants. When counsel wish to speak to the presiding judge in chambers during a trial they should not bring their ungowned assistants without asking the judge's permission. Similarly, when counsel are called into chambers the judge expects to see counsel only, not a cluster of law students and investigators. Again, you may ask leave to have them with you, but since I have never seen them play any role in such situations beyond that of mere spectators I wonder why you would. The informality that traditionally prevails between counsel and the judge in chambers is something to which a judge might not think it appropriate to expose others. Putting it another way, the tradition of confidentiality and informality that should prevail might be affected by the presence of persons who are not, as counsel are, officers of the court. So do not just stroll in with your entourage in tow. The judge might not say anything about it but you might not be asked back.

Bowing

This might be a good point to speak of bowing. It is yet another quaint tradition, like the wearing of gowns and tabs.

It is not intended to prove the superiority of the judge and the servility of the Bar. If that were so the judge would not bow back. It could be explained as a symbol of the reciprocal respect that exists between Bar and Bench, but I think it is just an old-fashioned way of greeting and parting, like shaking hands when we are not in court.

I have mentioned that some people dislike this old custom. If you feel that way, do not bow. The judge and everyone else will bow anyway; for anyone who has been much in the courts the habit is ingrained. Not much of a bow, as bows go, is required; no more than a nod of the head is necessary, though at least a slight forward inclination of the upper torso is customary.

There are those of the other conviction who love bowing. They are constantly bowing deeply from the waist like the imitation Japanese gentlemen in "The Mikado". Everytime you look at them they bow. Bowing need not include scraping. After a while the judge begins to feel as if he is watching Punch and Judy. As with everything good counsel do, discretion is the word.

My co-author had an experience that might be said to illustrate over-bowing. Here are his words:

> I was sitting in the Queen's Bench court room hearing motions when a prisoner escaped from the court room next door. He ran up behind the judge in that court room and ran out the door and then came bounding down the corridor and burst open the door behind me, ran around behind the dais and then through the court and out the door. He was pursued by two gaolers carrying handcuffs. They ran in front of me, stopped, bowed, and ran out the far door. I thought bowing in the circumstances was rather unnecessary.

He adds:

> It may be worth mentioning that although counsel paused during

the interruption, no one in the court room made any comment and the argument proceeded as if nothing whatever had happened.

Again, bowing is a custom of the court. Please do not bow to judges in the street; some are elderly and might faint. In court the tradition is to bow at the door when you are entering or leaving and when you take your place at the counsel table or leave it. Why one bows at the door I do not know, but it has been done as long as I have been around the courts. Judges vary in their bowing practice. Some bow at the beginning and end of the day but not during intervening recesses. Some bow whenever taking their place on the dais or leaving it. This can cause some hilarity. In one court in which I sit with two other judges, when the first to leave during a recess habitually bows he may be almost run over by the other two who are convinced non-bowers for recesses. In spite of such sources of confusion counsel customarily simply conform to the practice of the presiding judge.

The judge runs the court

Counsel must never address one another directly. Remarks, or questions, that counsel wish to direct to opposing counsel are put through the judge. Counsel do this even when answering a question that has been asked by another counsel. Thus, you do not turn to opposing counsel and say, "Do you intend to withdraw the claim in paragraph 7 of your statement of claim?" Counsel put such a question through the judge, as in "Perhaps, My Lord, my friend would tell us if he intends to withdraw the claim in paragraph 7 of his statement of claim?" The answer is also made to the judge, as in: "The answer is

No, My Lord, and I may add that my friend should have been aware of that", etc.

Note that other counsel are referred to as "my friend". Q.C.'s are referred to as "my learned friend". Counsel never refer to opposing counsel as "he" or "she". Oddly enough, there is nothing exceptionable about a presiding judge doing so.

Save when counsel are questioning witnesses or opening or closing to the jury, everything is addressed to the judge as, in Parliament, everything is addressed to the speaker. This avoids name-calling and shouting matches and gives the judge control of the court. Counsel never address ushers, or constables, or the court reporter directly. If counsel wish a lectern, or to have a witness called, or to have something read back by the reporter, they ask the judge, and if the judge approves he or she directs it to be done.

All of this points up the fact that the judge runs the court. This is something that others sometimes find surprising. I do not know how many times I have been told by court officials that "we don't do it that way". The answer to that is, "Oh yes we do". If that is what the judge wishes, and those wishes are legal, no one, not the registrar, nor the sheriff nor the Attorney General, nor anyone else can say him nay. Again, the point is not that the judge is so superior a person that others must defer obsequiously to his or her every whim. It is that the whole court system exists to facilitate the disposition of cases by judges. Judges do not need all the usual trappings of a court room; they can sit and hear cases outside under a tree if they like, for the judge *is* the court and wherever and whenever the judge sits to hear cases, there is the court. Thus it is that the living-room or front porch of a judge's summer cottage will serve just as well for the hearing of an urgent *ex parte* injunction application as will any court room. There is no magic about a court room; it is merely a place that has been set up in a certain pattern to facilitate the hearing of cases by judges and juries and to ensure public access to trials.

I am dwelling on this at perhaps too great length because during a murder trial at which I was presiding I was told at different times by the Crown attorney presenting the case, the deputy registrar and the sheriff's deputy assigned to protect me from the madding crowd, "We don't do it that way." I had just finished another murder trial in which defence counsel repeatedly told me the same thing. They all received a mild little lecture along the foregoing lines although the last recipient did not appear to think it was mild. Do not expose yourself to one like it.

Addressing the court or judge

One telling revelation of "dabbleritis" is failure to know the proper form of address for a court. The members of the court to which I belong are properly addressed, by a now quaint but ancient and established custom, as "My Lord" or "My Lady". Members of county and district courts are properly addressed as "Your Honour". Other courts have other traditional forms of address.

It should not take more than a moment to learn how to address a court, but it is surprising how frequently counsel appear who do not know it. Members of my court are frequently addressed in new and different ways. From counsel, "Your Honour" is fairly routine, as is "Your Honour, I mean My Lord", and I have had "Your Lord", "My Lordship", the female form being, I suppose, "Your Lady" or "My Ladyship". While no witness has ever conferred the title "Your Excellency" upon me I have heard reports of it (my co-author once experienced it from the sheriff, see Chapter 20) and I once had the excruciating experience of being called "Your Highness" by a nervous accused.

No doubt such things may be expected of witnesses who, in my experience at the Bar, generally found it almost beyond belief that anyone in Canada today should be addressed as "My Lord", or "My Lady", but I am not speaking here of dabbleritis among witnesses. Failure on the part of counsel to learn and follow the customary form of address for a court is as egregious as calling your physician "Mr.". It is the tell-tale mark of a dabbler and, since it is done in court in front of everyone, a signal to the world that you do not know what you are about. As for witnesses, all you can do is tell them how to address the court and hope for the best. Most of them will address the judge as "Your Honour" because that is what they have learned from television programs. I have not seen in Canada the device installed at the front of the witness box in the High Court in Nassau in the Bahamas. It is an ivory tablet, placed on the top rail on the witness box so as to be almost impossible to miss, and it says in big black letters, "Speak up and address the judge as My Lord". I wonder if it works.

I repeat that I am not defending the custom of addressing individuals in our society as "My Lord" and "My Lady". It is open to attack by rationalists and egalitarians. I am merely pointing out that it is yet another custom which to flout could do you harm. I have heard of lawyers who could not bring themselves to say "My Lord", and I understand their feelings. If you are one of those I think few judges would object to "Sir" or "Ma'am", although some strong traditionalists might.

Again, the risk is that you appear not to know the "right" way.

Outside court, or the precincts of court, "My Lord", "My Lady" or "Your Honour" is appropriate only at gatherings of judges and lawyers. To be addressed in that way at a ball game or a dance can be a bit of a jar. I think the English custom of informal address as "Judge" is acceptable here, as in "Good morning, Judge" when meeting on the street. On purely social occasions the form of address should reflect the relationship of the parties and the nature of the occasion.

When you introduce a superior court judge you should say, "I would like you to meet Mr. (or Madam) Justice Blank", whether the introduction is to a lawyer or a layman.

On more formal occasions the judge's full title is given, as in "The Honourable Mr. Justice Kindly", or, for a county or district court judge, "The Honourable Judge Worthy". If you are writing to a superior court judge you address the letter to "The Honourable Mr. Justice (or Madam Justice) Equable" and the recipient as "My Lord" or "My Lady" just as if you were in court. A letter to a member of a county or district court is addressed to "The Honourable Judge Wise" and the recipient as "Your Honour".

I am conscious that some of this might be dismissed as trivia and I regret the necessity for saying it, but so many young people have urged me to include it that I have ruefully acceded. Again, the problems stem from the break-down of the traditional method of training advocates through which one learned such obligatory niceties from those in the know.

Other people's customs

A word about other people's practices may not be amiss. There is nothing wrong with American customs, in the place where they belong. That place is the U.S.A., just as the customs of the Jamaican Bar are for Jamaica. We do not address high court judges as "M'Lud"; we say "My Lord" and so do English barristers in English courts, but in Jamaica they say "M'Lud". Nothing wrong with it, but we do not do it.

Thus, the customs and traditions I have been talking about are our own. They are not English customs and not American customs, although many might be common to all. We have developed strong court traditions. They might not be very different from others, but they are different, just as Americans might not be very different from Canadians but they are different.

The special concern that one must have for American customs is that they are so pervasive. We see trials depicted in American movies and on television, and read about them in American books and journals. The extent to which American symbols have crept into our consciousness is illustrated by the gavel. The gavel is an American symbol for the law. I have never seen a gavel used in a Canadian court. The only use I ever saw made of one in anything resembling a court in Canada was in a televised hearing before a university disciplinary tribunal. There the gavel was used by an eminent professor of law who presided over the hearing. He was an American who had taught for years in Canada and won a respected place here, but I doubt if he had ever seen the inside of a Canadian court room. The lawyers who saw that on television laughed to see him whacking the table with his gavel to try to maintain order. (The lawyers present at the hearing did not laugh: they maintained a respectful silence.)

Despite its complete absence from Canadian courts the gavel is used routinely in Canadian advertising to represent the law. I have a file of examples culled from newsapers, magazines and films. Among them is a flyer from one of the biggest and oldest Canadian law publishers announcing the publication of a new legal text. Surely they should know better! But before condemning them, consider that the huge advertising campaign mounted by the Ontario Attorney General's department to introduce a new system of courts featured a gavel as its central visual image!

I suppose the reason is that advertising people generally do not know how laughable it is to use the gavel as a symbol of law or court proceedings in Canada. Nor, for that matter, do many members of the public, inundated as they are by the ignorant advertisers. The typical gift made to a judge on his or her appointment to the Bench is, in my experience, a gavel. A colleague tells me he has three. There must be hundreds of gavels hidden away in judges' chambers in Canada. Certainly you do not see them used in court so they must be somewhere.

So consider the gavel before rushing to adopt other people's customs and symbols if you wish to make it appear that, as a Canadian counsel, you know what you are about. Begin calling other lawyers "counsellor" (as in "Good morning, counsellor") or refer to colleagues as "attorneys" (even the Crown attorney is referred to as "the Crown", not "the attorney"), begin being lippy with judges and calling news conferences in criminal cases to advertise your importance (or news conferences at all), put your witnesses "on the stand" instead of "in the box", say "strike that" to the court reporter, or "objection" to a judge, and you will reveal how little you know about Canadian courts and how much time you spend watching television. I have even had counsel say "May we approach the Bench?", to which I could only say "What for?". Approaching the Bench for a little off-the-record discussion between counsel and the judge is unheard of here; in our courts everything done in court must be on the record.

I hope no one reads this as decrying American customs. Some of them I think are better than some of ours. I am not comparing them unfavourably with ours; I am merely pointing out that they are out of place here. I am aware that many of them are a reflection of the egalitarian tradition that followed the War of Independence. That was illustrated for me in something said by a great and famous American counsel, John Shepherd of St. Louis. During a discussion he asked me what I meant by "juniors". I explained that juniors were assistants to a leading counsel. "Do you not have juniors?" I asked. "No," he said, "we don't have juniors, we just have wonderful guys."

Some essential skills

I have been talking about how counsel demonstrate their professionalism by knowing and adhering to the customs of the court but that is by no means the whole story. Sheer skill is the best proof. The professional skills peculiar to counsel work are more the subject of my co-author's discourse than mine. But there are a few common illustrations of lack of skill that will make you look pretty inept if you are not careful.

The most common and serious shortcoming in counsel is that they do not know what evidence has been given. That is a source of constant embarrassment. They are without the means to cross-examine and they cannot sum up at the end of the trial. They are constantly in danger of falling into that most grievous of errors, misquoting the evidence. Counsel who misquote evidence are to judges as are cattle-rustlers to ranchers; their crime is inexcusable. Judges depend absolutely on the reliability of counsel; indeed, it is better to be reliable than clever, and counsel who cannot be depended upon are on the way to being pariahs.

In any but the most brief or minor case counsel must have someone with them to note down the answers made when they are examining in chief or cross-examining. Counsel can note down opponents' examinations themselves if they wish; they are free to do so. But they cannot do the same for their own. A dependable law student can be invaluable. He or she can not only note down the evidence but run errands because counsel must not leave court except during adjournments. If they do not have an accurate note of the evidence they will find themselves in the predicament, as counsel did in a murder trial I heard, of having to say to a witness, in cross-examination, "I believe you said in your evidence in chief that the walls were covered with blood", only to have the witness retort, "I don't believe I said that". In theory, you can resort to the record, but what a cumbersome process that is while the court reporter tries to find one line among thousands! The judge, or opposing counsel, might help, but do not depend upon it. Opposing counsel might be pleased to see you floundering in front of the jury and the judge might not wish dependence to be placed on his or her own note of an important passage. In the incident I have described we sat for about five minutes — a long time in a silent court — while the reporter vainly tried to locate the answer in a thick stenopad containing two days of that witness's evidence. Finally, counsel had to give up and go on without it, having been flatly contradicted.

That you cannot keep notes of your own examinations was

illustrated for me vividly in another murder trial. It had been estimated to run for two weeks. Defence counsel attempted to write down all the answers he received on his cross-examinations. His tendency was to cross-examine at length, and the long pauses between an answer and the next question ultimately had the predictable effect on judge and jury: they ran out of patience. Counsel felt the resulting pressure and had to abandon the practice. When he summed up for the jury he made several mistakes in reviewing the evidence, some of which were so flagrant that I felt obliged to correct them in my charge. That did little for him or his cause, for the correct versions, which I instructed the reporter to read back, were seriously adverse to his client's interests.

Another essential skill is to learn how to keep your temper. There are plenty of opportunities to lose it. When you do you lose your balance and impair your judgment. You become personally involved and the cause becomes yours: it is no longer your client's. There is an old adage that says a man is likely to be a fool in his own cause. If you have an incurably bad temper and cannot cure it you should stay out of court. I have never seen counsel lose their temper in court and not look foolish.

For the benefit of those who are not aware of the significance of these lines I should add that, as the inheritor of a family tradition of quick tempers, I should know. I fear my first days at the Bar proved the worth of the advice I have just given and thus I know whereof I speak. Again, it was the red-headed and quick-tempered Walter Williston who taught me that a bad temper was an almost fatal defect in counsel; even if he or she survives at the Bar it will not be with any friends. Williston taught himself how to curb his temper and, fortunately for me, helped me with mine. While I might never have graduated from his course in self-control, at least I was able to see how futile and babyish my habit made me appear and how ruinous it was for my cause.

It is a mark of bad counsel to abuse witnesses. That is bad manners but, worse, there is no quicker or surer way to alienate a judge or jury. Sometimes, very, very rarely, a witness is so patently unresponsive, devious or contemptuous that he or she earns and deserves abuse. Everyone then enjoys watching the witness being taught that one cannot get away with that in court, but before embarking on teaching such a lesson you must be very, very sure that it is justified.

When it is justified, it can be devastating. I once saw the following done by Williston. In a domestic fight that turned on credibility, the husband had testified about his income. Williston, for the wife, "smelled a rat", as he put it. With leave of the judge he took the husband's income tax returns, which had been entered as exhibits, out of court to study overnight. He found that they very seriously contradicted the husband's testimony, and, as well, appeared to be false. The next morning Williston continued his cross-examination. Carefully he led up to the point where the husband had to admit that they were false but suggested that the wife had been an accomplice. It sounded almost plausible. In an unusual gesture, Williston walked up to the witness, looked him in the eye and said, very softly, "Sir, I suggest to you that you are a liar." He walked away and sat down.

The husband just gaped. The judge — one known for his compassion and fairness — sat silent. The husband's counsel leapt to his feet. So unnerved was he that he disassociated himself from his client's testimony. The result was ruinous for the husband's case.

I have never seen anything quite so effective since then, but

I have seen many witnesses called liars and in almost every case I thought, and I have reason to think the jury thought, that the comment was unjustified and unfair. So be careful. Knowing what to do and when to do it is the key to success as counsel.

The best counsel seem to know instinctively what to do. They don't bumble or stall with an eye on the clock hoping to run the day out in order to get a chance to think of what to do; they just go for it. Yet what looks to be instinct is mostly experience. They did not all start off as winners. Some of them had little apparent talent and atrocious manners but, being serious about their craft, they quickly learned.

They did not learn by being taught how to do it by judges. Ever since a well-meaning judge was pilloried in the press for telling a lawyer that white socks were out of place in court, the general style among judges has been to sit quietly and let lawyers make spectacles of themselves.

Making it to the top

I said earlier that a barrister's reputation is made or lost in court. It is extremely important that you know your case and the law, but it is equally important that you appear to know the ropes. It breeds confidence and respect. Again, I do not pause to examine why that is but simply recognize that it is. If you want to be a member of the top group you have to look as if you belong, and to do this you must know your way around.

This is true in other walks of life, of course. A lawyer was once having lunch with a client. He had taken the client to lunch because the client had just missed a big promotion, and knew it. He was bitter that he, as a senior company officer, had participated in the firing of the president, whose job he had reasonably expected would be his, and about the unfairness of his situation when compared with the departed president, whose way out had been greatly eased by a "golden hand-shake". "Is there a presidents' club?" he inquired plaintively. The answer could not be given but, yes, there is a presidents' club, and so is there a counsel's club, an inner circle of top counsel who recognize each other, recommend each other, and share briefs with each other. You will know when you have made it into the charmed circle and it will give you a very satisfactory feeling. It is also good in other ways: almost all the big cases are handled by the top counsel. All of them should be, but because the top counsel and their firms cannot possibly represent everyone, or because of competing interests or affiliations, they must frequently send their clients to other counsel. Thus, the best work is passed around this golden circle and the rewards of being recognized as a member are not confined to self-esteem.

CHAPTER 11

PERSONAL MANNERISMS

IRRITATING PERSONAL mannerisms can severely interfere with your effectiveness in court. The reason is that they are distracting. Counsel who tap pencils incessantly on the counsel table, who point fingers at judges, rap rulers on the witness box, walk restlessly about when examining, interrupt, mumble, snicker, chew gum, smirk, converse at the counsel table while opposing counsel are examining witnesses, rush questions at witnesses or fail to wait for answers, sit, or slouch, while speaking or being spoken to, all run the risk of irritating the judge or jury and distracting attention from a good cause to a bad performance.

It can, of course, be hilarious. The tale is told of one much loved counsel who was summing up for the jury in a case in which two boys had been rabbit hunting and one shot the other. The jurors watched intently but with increasing bewilderment as counsel rushed around the well of the court, adopting the presumed attitudes of the hunters in an attempt to demonstrate how easily the "accident", as the defence saw it, could have occurred. Finally, the judge had to intervene. He stopped counsel in mid-crouch and said, "Mr. Walsh, would you mind telling us whether you are, at this moment, the boy who was shot, or the boy who shot him, or the rabbit."

For a judge to make a comment upon even the most irritating mannerisms is probably rare. For the most part judges just sit patiently trying to ignore them, and to follow the evidence or the argument. Some are not easy to ignore. One counsel, exceptionally talented in other ways, had a curious habit of reacting to questions from the Bench by holding up his hand like an imitation pistol, with forefinger pointed and thumb cocked, aiming it at the judge and saying, "Chuff, Chuff," as if firing. Another able counsel is known to some as "the finger" from his habit of fixing judges with a glittering eye and pointing menacingly at them, as one might at a pet dog to emphasize one's demand to be obeyed.

I think few people could continue to concentrate objectively on the evidence or the argument while this kind of thing is going on, and, as I have said before, it is useful to keep in mind that judges are people. No one of intelligence would set out to harm his cause by irritating the very person he hopes to persuade. The key to the problem of why it is done must be found elsewhere than in intention.

The answer is, in my opinion, that those afflicted are simply not aware of it. Surely, sniffers, twitchers, blinkers, knuckle-crackers, hawkers, theatre-seat kickers and all such people with mild to monstrously irritating mannerisms are not conscious of them. Did the young counsel I once watched perform realize that not once did he look at any witness he was questioning, and very rarely at me when speaking to me, preferring to keep his gaze fixed on the line behind us where the court room wall met the ceiling? I think not.

It is possible to lecture to a class or an audience and keep one's eye fixed on the chandelier and get away with it, for the task might not involve the need to persuade anyone of anything and the teacher's tenure will not suffer. It is said that Burke "spoke to history" rather than to the House of Commons, and he certainly got away with it. But counsel's task is a more immediate one: it is to persuade his audience then and there that his cause is right and just. Surely no one with that in mind would *consciously* do anything that would spoil his chances of success.

In emphasizing the word "consciously" I can again claim to know whereof I speak. My first lesson stemmed from an appearance I made in the Supreme Court of Canada. Failing vision had led me to wearing spectacles. I favoured the "Ben Franklin" type then in vogue, black plastic half-moons used for reading, with straight temples that gripped the head rather than curl around the ears. The trouble with them was that, with use, their grip relaxed and they tended to fall off the nose when one bent forward. After the hearing I happened to meet one of the members of the court on the street. We were friends of long standing. He told me that the court had been "fascinated", his word, with my presentation. I had little reason to think it had been my best performance and modestly inquired what he meant. He explained, "You were having a little trouble with your glasses. When you were looking up at us there was no problem but when you looked down to read they nearly always slipped off. Your right hand came up automatically, caught them, and put them back on your nose. You never paused, glanced at the glasses nor looked away from the book. We were simply fascinated. It was a remarkable example of reflex action."

I thanked him sincerely. Only a friend with my interests at heart would have told me such an embarrassing story, but he was such. His name was Bora Laskin. Before throwing those glasses as far as I could into the Ottawa River I found myself thinking about two things: the first was that until then I was not aware that I had acquired such a distracting habit; the second was that it was no wonder that the court had dismissed my appeal from the Bench without calling on the other side. They probably didn't hear a word I said!

My second lesson was administered by a friend and client, who asked my wife to see if on a proposed trip she could "buy some rubber money" for me. When I asked her to explain she said he could no longer stand my habit of turning my coins in my pocket. As she had reached the same point she did not hesitate to pass the suggestion along. Astounded, I learned that I had become known for this habit, that during long meetings and conferences I did it incessantly and that it drove most people to distraction.

I learned something else from that experience. Since they could all hear the coins being turned and I could not it was clearly time for a visit to an ear specialist.

These experiences lead me to believe that most possessors of irritating mannerisms are not conscious of them or of their effect on others. That makes it difficult to correct them but, if you are the unfortunate possessor of such an affliction, correct it you must.

I have said that the problem is that they are distracting. Judges try hard to follow the case. Even at the best of times that requires total concentration. It is not only counsel who are worn out after a day in court. The attempt to follow, weigh and understand evidence and argument and to make coherent notes is always demanding and can be exhausting. Trying to follow a frightened, reluctant or incoherent witness can be an almost impossible task when counsel are conducting a side-show at the counsel table, sharing witticisms, tapping with pencils, snapping binders open and shut, or, when examining, striding around the court room as if on a walking tour.

How do you cure yourself? The answer is that you cannot if

you are unaware that you have a problem. Nor can you depend upon family or friends, who might prefer to avoid embarrassing you or receiving an angry retort. Anger is a common response to kindly attempts to cure people of embarrassing defects they do not know they have. Judges are not likely to mention it to you, for ever since the "white socks" affair (mentioned earlier in this chapter) judges of my acquaintance have preferred to avoid comment on counsel's personal idiosyncrasies. Opposing counsel cannot be relied upon for advice; they may be delighted with your performance. No one in court — opponents, juniors, ushers, judges, jurors — will tell you of your bad habits. There are only two ways that I know of to discover them. One is to have a friend, who is sufficiently concerned for your welfare to be honest with you, watch your court performance and appraise it frankly. The other way is to develop a sense of self-awareness keen enough to reveal your faults to yourself. That can be an immeasurably invaluable skill in any walk of life, but of the two methods the latter is probably the less reliable.

CHAPTER 12

DROOPY TAB SYNDROME
AND "GAPOSIS"

SUCCESSFUL COUNSEL look successful. They look the part. They do not wear crumpled gowns or soiled linen. They do not display a stretch of electric-blue or tartan skirt or trouser between waistcoat and shoes. They do not suffer from "gaposis" — a slash of bulging white shirt across the abdomen between vest and belt buckle. Their gowns fit; they are neat and clean; they look as if they mean business.

If you do not believe this go to court and watch the good counsel. You will see exceptions, but the exceptions are so good at their job that they can afford to ignore the dress code a little. They do not ignore it much. Walter Williston was sometimes a little rumpled, but everyone knew he had probably been up all night honing his argument. You will be permitted to play with the standards a little when you are that good.

I do not propose to analyse the connection between proper dress and success, but it is there. One judge has a test. It is called "droopy-tab syndrome". When he sees counsel in a set of wrinkled, floppy, soiled tabs he makes a mental note born of long experience: do not expect much from this one. He is not always right, but you would be surprised at how often he is, as he was when he discovered it. (Another judge once called counsel into his chambers and *gave* him a set of clean tabs.)

It is easy, when you are new in court, to miss the point of proper dress. Uniforms have been given a bad name by the jeans generation. Some uniforms are thought elitist (private schools), some snobbish (dinner-jackets), some as destroyers of individuality (the military). People who come to the Bar with such thoughts have trouble accommodating to its old-fashioned ways. They think that gowns and dark or striped trousers or skirts are intimidating, an imposition, a threat to their freedom of expression. They conform with an ill-will and as little as possible.

They are missing the point. The point is, admittedly, obscure. One can hardly blame them. It takes a little looking into.

First, everyone who works for a living in the courts has a distinctive dress: judge, clerk, sheriff's deputy, constable, counsel. All those uniforms have their own story. I am concerned here only with the dress of counsel, but it is worth noticing that not only counsel are in uniform. Everyone has his own role; everyone has his own dress.

Next, you will notice that barristers' gowns tend to make all barristers look alike. It diminishes the differences among them. From the clothes barristers wear a layman or juror would have trouble telling the struggling newcomer from the successful and rich old hand. There is a difference between Q.C.s' and non-Q.C s' gowns but to laymen it is imperceptible.

Thus, gowns make every pleader equal at the Bar. It does not matter if your clothes are custom made or off-the-rack, or if they make you look like a captain of industry or the office mouse. Everyone looks the same. What makes one stand out from the others is the quality of his or her advocacy, not of his or her clothes.

Gowns mean also that you do not have to worry about "what to wear?" Over your lifetime you are going to have to think about that a lot, whether you like it or not, and if you do not someone else will be doing it for you. It has always been, and it will always be, that different occasions require different dress: the most resolute individualist would not wear jeans to a formal wedding. But you do not have to worry about what to wear to court: the gown is "right". You can put the time you might spend on tie selection into working on your case.

If that sounds somewhat unreal consider the situation where gowns are not worn. In the U.S.A. counsel are not gowned, even though the judges are. The problem the absence of gowns causes for lawyers generated the career of "America's first wardrobe engineer", John T. Molloy. In his best-selling book, "Dress for Success", Mr. Molloy tells how he got his start. It was advising New York law firms on "proper attire for a lawyer in the court room". He had many customers.

So there you are: there are many reasons for the wearing of gowns and few against it. The traditional uniforms of the courts are perpetuated in the interest of getting on with the job with as little distraction as possible. Oddly enough, the barrister's gown sometimes generates distraction. Far from resisting the gown, some people revel in it, swooping and dipping around court like ballet dancers. I remember John J. Robinette, Q.C., once protesting to a trial judge in a hard-fought case in a small town before a crowd of spectators that "his friend", my senior, was distracting the witness by "switching his tail around the court like a peacock". The switching stopped.

So remember Mr. Molloy, and the thousands of barristers who have preceded you, and decide to "dress for success". Competition at the Bar is becoming too keen to let dress give an advantage to the other side.

CHAPTER 13

KEEP YOUR FACE STRAIGHT

APART FROM BEING a test of determination and skill a trial is a performance put on for a judge or jury. It is a very serious affair. It is not done for the judge's amusement; it is done to persuade him or her of the rightness of a cause. The techniques of persuasion include the visual. People tend to believe in a person who appears to believe in himself. Judges and juries are not immune to real sincerity and confidence on the part of counsel. Thus, "how it looks" is important.

Counsel are watched, it is said, "from the time they enter the court room" but in fact they are watched all the time. How counsel act in the corridor can be important. Foolish antics or gestures seen by jurors outside the court room might create a suspicion in a juror that counsel is not serious about his case. That can be very bad.

Counsel must never let their case down by any action or gesture in or out of court that shows a lack of confidence or sincerity. Above all, in court counsel must control their facial expressions. A witness may give an answer that is disastrous to the questioner yet the questioner must not appear to be aware his case has suffered a blow. That is important: the weight of the blow may escape the judge or the jury who, after all, do not know as much as counsel does about his case and may therefore miss the significance of the answer. Remember that judge and jury are watching not only the witness but counsel. An answer may be given that makes them wonder, but unless its significance is signalled by some gesture or reaction on the part of counsel the fact that the answer is a blow to counsel's case may be lost on them.

Thus, keep your face straight. Not only that: you must not allow those on your side of the case to give an indication that the case is in trouble. You must thus ensure that clients and witnesses do not betray concern. If clients or witnesses sitting in court cannot keep a straight face then measures should be taken which include keeping them out of court. You must therefore try to be aware of what is happening behind your back — the judge can see it even if you cannot.

The same applies to others with you at the counsel table. One great counsel, now a judge, refused to have a law student or an assisting counsel sit with him at the counsel table for fear that their face might reflect bad answers or incipient disasters. That great man was extremely sensitive to the effect his case was having on a jury. Since most of his practice consisted of defending murder cases he had learned to read the faces of the jury. All the jury ever read in his face, however, was quiet confidence and sincerity. Because he could not control the faces and the actions of those assisting him he would have no one associated with his case near him during a trial unless he could be absolutely certain they would follow his example.

Walter Williston was a student of how other counsel handled disaster. A disastrous answer could occur in chief or in cross-examination, either when he was on his feet or sitting at the counsel table. He came to know that he had struck hard when certain counsel smiled. He knew that because that is what he had taught himself to do when his case was hurt in order to conceal his horror. Such was his skill that he discovered that certain counsel smiled *only* when their case had been dealt a blow. Lest others learn the same of him he taught himself to introduce — with a little smile — an occasional touch of humour. That concealed the effect of his smiling at disaster and was a test of other counsel's reactions.

Other trial counsel, less accomplished than Williston, gave away their hand at sometimes only slight provocation. One could tell when they were hit by the pain they displayed. The most common of these revealing reactions, one that is seen every day in courts today and which is still the least effective, was bluster. Jumping up to protest and interrupt a cross-examination is an almost sure-fire way to reveal the hurt to one's case. Attempting to "rescue" a witness by that crude tactic is a dead give-away.

Williston saved his deepest admiration for one counsel who had total control of his facial muscles. Williston used to say, "If the roof blew off the court house you would never know it by watching Roly." It followed that if the roof blew off Williston's case his face would not reveal it.

CHAPTER 14

SPEAK UP!

A COURT ROOM frequently is a place with poor acoustics presided over by a person with poor hearing. If you want to win, or if you merely want to be heard, speak up!

Judges can be touchy about their hearing. Deafness is to many part of the stereotype of cranky old age. Every one has heard about elderly patriarchs of the Bench who removed their ear trumpets to avoid hearing an argument they disliked. Judges might look old to you, but most of them do not feel old and many go to great lengths to conceal their hearing problems.

Perhaps for this reason judges are not likely to tell you more than once that they cannot hear you, so it is a good idea to speak louder than you think necessary. They will certainly tell you if you are speaking too loudly, but in thirty-five years in court I have never heard any judge tell counsel that.

Remember that the judge you are addressing is likely to be older than you are and that hearing acuity declines with age. The general age bracket for judges is about 40 to 70. The general age bracket for counsel is 30 to 55.

You might be surprised to know that in the judges' age group poor hearing might be more common than poor sight. In *A Good Age*, that excellent book by Dr. Alex Comfort,[1] the author tells us that 29 per cent of people over 65 have hearing loss, far more than have bad sight. The problem may

---

[1]New York, Simon and Shuster, 1976.

be more acute for women counsel because, according to Dr. Comfort, hearing loss is likely to be more acute in the upper register, a more common range for women's voices than for men's.

You might well ask why does a judge who is hard of hearing not wear a hearing aid? The answer is that many do, but for those with hearing that is still fairly good a hearing aid can seem more trouble than it is worth. So they prefer to go on without one.

Books have recently been published that illustrate vividly why court room acoustics are so bad. They show pictures of old court houses that are a reflection of Canada's growing interest in its past. According to the foreword to one of the best of these, more than half of the buildings shown were built before 1850. Only a few were built in this century. The oldest still in use was built in 1824. They are mostly Georgian or Victorian and built in a style intended to express the ebullient confidence of our forefathers. Succeeding generations have thought them to be ugly, but now the tendency is to classify them as "of significant historical interest", or, at least, quaint. Some were, and are, simply beautiful. Some of the loveliest have the worst acoustics. One gracious old structure I have presided in has a high ceiling and glass dome that for some reason makes it less easy to hear the witnesses than the pigeons cooing on the roof.

It is pleasant to have these links with our past but their acoustics are generally terrible. The court rooms tend to be all hard surfaces: sound-reflecting polished wood benches and wainscoting, linoleum floors, plaster walls and ceilings. A book dropped in one corner will make people in another corner jump.

Some efforts have been made to improve the acoustics of these old rooms. What is done seems to depend on the wishes of the local judge, many of whom have had to sacrifice tradition to practicality. Thus, you will see grey-white acoustic tile glued up walls and across ceilings: horribly desecrating to the proud and stern look of the old room but, no doubt, necessary to the preservation of the judge's temper, or even sanity.

New court rooms are not always built with a sufficient concern for acoustics but most are better than their predecessors. One of the best is so good it calls to mind a story.

In almost the first case heard there counsel were, as usual, talking among themselves at the counsel table. What was different was that the judge could hear them. They did not realize that because in the court rooms of the Victorian structure they had practised in for so long they could talk among themselves without fear of being overheard. Some of their comments on this occasion were about the judge. I will not repeat them here. The judge finally said, "Gentlemen, may I suggest that when you have anything to say about me in this court you put it in a note and pass it to each other. I have heard everything you have said."

You might keep in mind a formula: the likelihood that you will not be heard increases with the age of the court house and the age of the judge.

For these reasons you might agree with me that a soft voice is counsel's curse. It is impossible to get to the top at the Bar without a voice capable of carrying you there. Most of the top counsel appear to have been born with a firm, loud voice (no doubt some have deliberately developed one). If you listen carefully you will find that they tend to have a certain timbre; a carrying quality that is produced without strain. It does not follow that the voices are all attractive; some are harsh, some are nasal, some rasping, but one can hear them.

Those who are born with easily heard voices are lucky. They do not have to suffer people telling them all their lives to speak up. It is possible that mumblers are made, not born. They mumble in retaliation against people who are constantly telling them to speak up. For a child with a quiet voice life seems to be a succession of authority figures: parents, teachers, uncles and aunts, grandparents, etc., all shouting, "Speak up, I can't hear you." Once formed, the mumbling habit is hard to break. Mumblers are like donkeys. Shouting at a mumbler produces only more mumbling. Mumblers believe that when they raise their voices to an audible level people will think they are shouting. The only sure cure for mumbling is voice therapy. A mumbler must either choose that or find a place where he can earn a living by mumbling, if there is one.

The importance of a clear, easily audible voice cannot be over-stated. A strong, clear voice conveys power, authority and conviction. No one could be long in the same court room with the late Arthur Patillo, Q.C., without feeling the strength that his enormous voice gave to his wispy figure. The late John Diefenbaker had a legendary success while still a young man at the criminal bar. He was a man of powerful personality, but it can hardly be doubted that the power of his voice added much to his power to persuade. While we are on the subject, remember that when God himself is portrayed in the movies it is usually by way of an unseen presence with an enormous voice.

The old rule for public speakers is, stand up, speak up, shut up. Above all, speak up.

CHAPTER 15

THE RUDE JUDGE AND THE
TAKE-OVER JUDGE

ALL THE TALK of manners in counsel is all very well, you might say, but what of judges? Are they immune? If not, why are there ill-mannered, short-tempered, pushy judges? Why should they be allowed to get away with it if counsel are not?

Yes, there are crabby, ill-mannered, bad-tempered judges. There always have been. Stories abound of the spectacular rudeness of the Ontario Court of Appeal in the Thirties. The judges were not just rude to counsel; they were rude to each other. Those stories will have to keep for another time; they are not appropriate here. No less an expert witness than John J. Robinette, Q.C., has testified to the general improvement in judges' manners. In an address given in 1983, he said:

> Some aspects of the profession have changed for the better. When I was a very young lawyer there were a few rude judges on the Supreme Court of Ontario particularly when young counsel were appearing before them. Today all of that is gone and judicial manners have improved and our Court of Appeal and our trial judges today are men and women of courtesy and thoughtfulness.

That is pleasant to hear, but there are still occasions when judicial manners fall below acceptable levels. We all hear of them. They are an embarrassment to everyone. But to counsel who have to deal with them they are more than that: they are a test of skill.

88

You cannot win a contest of rudeness with a judge. If the judge interrupts unnecessarily or unfairly, displays hostility to you or your cause, appears to have made up his or her mind before hearing you, brow-beats you or your witnesses, you have only one course of action open: stand your ground. Do that with firmness, but also with courtesy. Judges are allowed some latitude, the better to enable them to conduct or to understand the case before them. But the limits are exceeded when a judge steps out of the judge's role. The judge's job is to sit and listen and decide. He or she may ask questions, but only for assistance in performing that role and not to assist or oppose counsel. The judge must not descend into the pit.

It is very easy to advise on what to do when the judge steps beyond the limit, but when it happens to you sage advice might be hard to remember. Emotions can rise rapidly in court notwithstanding the customary decorum and sober atmosphere. When you are subjected to rudeness from the Bench, hang on. It is a useful device to remember that it is all being taken down by the court reporter, and that your courtesy and controlled demeanour will stand you in good stead in the Court of Appeal. For some reason, unpleasant incidents that occur at trial do not lose their bite when written down; they actually look worse on paper.

One of today's leading cousel remembers some early advice he was given by his senior, Walter Williston. It was simply to take the abuse, knowing that it was all being taken down, but if it became unbearable say only "I submit that Your Lordship is being unfair". He has had to say it only twice in twenty-five years. On both occasions it was read with devastating effect in the Court of Appeal.

Happily, such occasions are rare. But if you would like to

learn from some real-life examples of how to deal with the problem, read *J.M.W. Recycling Inc. v. Attorney General of Canada*[1] and *Baker v. Hutchinson et al.*[2] There you will find exemplary displays of restraint, courtesy and firmness by counsel facing severe provocation. In the Court of Appeal, you will note, the wrongs were righted.

The rude judge can be a minor problem compared to the take-over judge. The latter wants to run your case for you. It does not matter if you are plaintiff or defendant but it is more likely to happen if you are plaintiff. Like the rude judge, the species is fairly rare but when encountered can be pretty daunting.

Take-over judges interrupt; they criticize you for calling witnesses, or for not calling witnesses; they make it plain that they would have run your case very differently and that what you are doing is a disservice to your client. In short, they try to take over counsel's role.

I have great sympathy for them. They are merely trying to help! I accept completely that they are probably attempting only to achieve a just result for the contestants and that their motives are impeccable. It is very hard to sit there and do nothing when inside a voice is screaming that counsel is dropping his or her case down the drain. Not all judges can contain themselves. Some give in to temptation and try to take over.

Whether their perception of the conduct of the case is right or wrong does not matter. I think that take-over judges tend towards incorrect perception because their judgment becomes clouded by their anxiety and they lose patience. As with the ordeal before the rude judge, you cannot win. Your chances of

---

[1] (1982), 35 O.R. (2d) 355, 133 D.L.R. (3d) 363.
[2] (1976), 13 O.R. (2d) 591 at pp. 596-7, 1 C.P.C. 291 at pp. 297-8.

winning on appeal, with costs, are, of course, strong, but it is unlikely you can turn the tables at trial. A leading counsel, and wit, once opened his remarks at a dinner to mark the retirement of a famous judge who suffered from a tendency to take over: "I have never won a case against Mr. Justice X". If such judges would only sit and wait they might see the plan. But right or wrong as they may be in their perception of how the case is being conducted, they are fatally wrong in trying to take it over. Do not let their error beget one of yours. Keep your fingers crossed and think of the record, for the technique of dealing with both types is the same. Keep your temper, stand your ground, be courteous and keep saying to yourself, "All this is being taken down and it always looks worse on paper."

Courts of appeal are not wholly immune from these foibles. You can have some fairly rough rides there, but remember one further thing: courts of appeal are not tolerant of take-over trial judges. Read *Phillips et al. v. Ford Motor Co. of Canada Ltd. et al.*,[3] where the interventions of a well-meaning and exceptionally skilled trial judge were thought by the Court of Appeal to have gone too far. It should be of assistance to you in a similar situation.

3[1971] 2 O.R. 637, 18 D.L.R. (3d) 641.

CHAPTER 16

WINNING AND LOSING

POPULAR JOURNALISM about great criminal counsel dwells on how many necks were saved by their advocacy. True, winning hard cases is not possible without care and skill. Yet all good counsel put the same amount of effort into the ones they lose. The higher you go up the counsel ladder the harder the cases become. No one thinks he needs a great counsel for a simple case or a "sure winner". It is the difficult cases that go to top counsel. The result is that even the greatest cannot win them all.

Think for a moment about the legendary greats. Of the hundreds of cases they appeared in how many have they won? A lot, no doubt, yet no one knows, and no one cares. The reason is that counsel do not become great counsel, or even good counsel, because of the number of cases they have won, or fail because of the number they have lost. There is no tally kept. Counsel X is not better than counsel Y because he has won 15 more cases over his lifetime than Y. What counts is how well he performed in every case.

Win or lose, you, as counsel, are performing for an audience from whose opinion will come your reputation. The judge hearing a case tells other judges if you were good. He or she will not bother to mention it if you were bad, unless you were very, very bad. The jury tell their friends. Counsel with or opposed to you, counsel waiting to come on, witnesses, court officials are impressed by how well you performed, not whether you won or lost. The court room is your stage. A great effort is great, win or lose.

As for the personal effect of winning or losing on established counsel, by and large their egos do not require a string of victories. They are tough enough to withstand a string of losses. The fact is that they do not have much time to think about it, for the end of one case simply means the beginning of another.

Thus, no one can win them all. Even when losing a case you can be winning a reputation. A lucky win will not add to your reputation; a loss after a hard and well-fought contest will. Always remember that, to misquote slightly a well-known couplet, it matters not that you won or lost, but how you played the game.

CHAPTER 17

WHY BOTHER?

WHY STRIVE FOR success as an advocate? Why work day and night for years, missing sleep, cancelling holidays at the last moment, lunching on sandwiches in the court house while your stomach churns, pushing through an unremitting blizzard of cases, trying to pick up the technology of air pollution for one case and the reason why new roofs leak for another; spending all day in court and most of the night preparing for next day; saying hello to the group of people involved in the next case before finding time to say goodbye to those in the last? Why work harder and longer than the office lawyers seem to? (Don't they always seem to be going to lunch, playing golf with clients and attending tax deductible conventions with their wives in exotic places?) Why put up with ungrateful clients who think that if you won it must have been easy and if you lost you must have been stupid, and office-bound colleagues who appear to regard what goes on in court as little more than a series of card tricks? Why not opt for a cozier life in the office with regular hours, less anxiety and a predictable timetable? In short: Why bother trying to get to the top of the advocacy ladder?

The answer for some is that they are temperamentally un-suited to any other kind of life. They are born combatants. They like action and gaining attention. Court fulfils their need for excitement and challenge, their desire, like tennis

94

players, to test themselves against better adversaries. The urgency of court work, the sudden triumphs and let-downs, the independence, the calls made on strength and resourcefulness, the very uncertainty of it all, keeps them on their toes and their adrenalin surging. To them court is life. They would fall asleep in an office. They did not choose court, it chose them.

Others have no choice for a different reason. Court work is what the office has for them to do, and it is either do that or leave.

For the rest, whose choice is imposed neither by temperamental imperative nor by economic necessity, the question whether to go into counsel work or into corporate, estate, or any other kind of work can be simply a matter of impulse, or it may be the result of much deliberation. Some do decide to give it a try without thinking or knowing much about it. They are likely to leave quickly and quietly after their first cold bath. It requires more than impulse to keep most people in court. Whatever the reasons that lead people into court, the fact is that they are not usually strong enough to push them up the ladder to the top. Fairly weak convictions may suffice to keep some people drifting around in court work in some middle ground between near-incompetence and real success. They get away with it because *there are never enough good counsel*. That is a fact. It is so today; it was so yesterday; it will always be so. That is one reason why so many second-raters find employment in the courts. There are not enough good counsel to go round.

There is always room at the top. A determined, sustained effort maintained over the years will not be in vain. The question is, is it worth it? What does success amount to?

My observation tells me that success as counsel is a real thing. You know when you have it — you can feel it. But it means different things to different people. It brings things like more independence, better control over your life, the luxury of choosing cases that interest you. Some like the attention of the news media. The big names at the top send briefs to you that they cannot handle because they are too busy, or because there is a conflict of interest or for some other reason. The consciousness that you have joined an elite and never large group does much for your self-esteem. Success brings big incomes. It may be that the barrister is not the stereotype of a saver. There is an old line about English counsel: "Barristers work hard, live well and die poor". But save or not, at and near the top counsel's incomes are high.

Success at the Bar also lends a hand to those who would clamber on to the Bench. It is true that some have been appointed from other fields of law, and they have proven mostly to be very good judges. Success as counsel does not guarantee success on the Bench, but it is the traditional way to get there. You have only to glance at the list of judges to see that nearly all were successful counsel.

What about failure? There is a risk to counsel work. It is possible to be a spectacular success. It is possible as well to be a spectacular failure: there have been some. When you fail you do it publicly. Some counsel have blown a lifetime's effort in one disastrous case. But most of those who fail do so more quietly and in a different sense. They just do not see the point of going on and they have the luxury of choice, so they drop out of court. They might regret that or they might not, but they are no doubt better lawyers for the experience they have had in court. They will be better office lawyers, better value to clients, because they have been at the heart of the system and have seen how it works. They may become "occasional barristers" and will be the better for their experience. Thus, any experience of counsel work is better than none. I think that every lawyer should give it a try. It will help immeasurably his or her understanding of the law.

PART II

THE ADVOCATE AT TRIAL

CHAPTER 18

PAPER

Preparation of documents for discovery, production, pre-trial and trial

WHILE "PAPER" IS only one chapter in this book, the failure to do the paperwork will mean that the techniques or tools that follow cannot be used effectively. Paper may be the bane of counsel, but disorganized paper may be the death of the case for counsel and the client.

Right from the first interview you must impress upon your client the absolute necessity of giving you every scrap of paper that could in any way be relevant to the case.

Pleadings, interlocutory motions, examinations for discovery and pre-trial conferences are generally beyond the scope of this book. We are discussing here what the trial judge sees and hears. Any trial judge can quickly recognize a prepared case as distinguished from one in which reams of loosely scattered papers have been lightly dusted the night before trial.

As the documents are collected you start your copying and indexing. You should copy the original documents and work from the copies. The original documents should be kept separate from the file and stored away to prevent loss and alteration. It is surprising how often an original document is filed as an exhibit with underlining, question marks, highlighting, etc. In a large case the original documents should only be removed from the original document file upon the signature of the recipient.

Documents should be indexed in chronological order. You may start with a thousand documents, so you number them from 1 to 1000. I see nothing wrong with putting your index number at the top right hand corner of the document. Each document should have its own file folder with its own code number. The file folders should be colour coded, for example, red, so that everyone working on the case or in your office knows that the folder contains an original document. As further documents are received they are fitted in in chronological order and they become, for example, document numbers 501A, 530A, 530B, etc. Documents for which you claim privilege should be marked with a separate code initial, for example, document number P301.

As the case progresses the documents will pick up extra numbers which will show in your index after your code number. These extra numbers will come from your affidavit on production number, your opponent's affidavit on production number, the exhibit numbers on discovery and finally the trial exhibit number. But always file your documents under your own code number. Sometimes it is helpful to cross-index documents under subject matter.

You must also cross-index the documents to your own code number so that, for example, when opposing counsel asks at trial for your affidavit on production number 36 you will know from your cross-index that this is your code number 140. You will be able to find and produce the document without delay.

Remember that many cases are won and lost on the documents. Judges like to rely on documents and often prefer the evidence of documents to a fallible memory.

It is your obligation as counsel to make full production, and it is also your obligation to see that you get full production from the other side. Insist on a complete affidavit of documents. In using the word "documents" I include photographs, plans, tape recordings, etc.

In a very complicated case with many documents you may consider the use of a computer. Perhaps you should retain assistance to set up computer programs for the storage and retrieval of documents. Computers have other uses in litigation, for example, the assembly of the evidence dealing with the main points involved. I doubt that any judge would object to the installation of a computer terminal in the court room.

Before you get to trial and even pre-trial you must decide on the documents that you wish to adduce in evidence. It is at this stage that you should co-operate with opposing counsel. You have already had an opportunity of examining each other's documents. He or she should gather his or her documents together, you should meet, go over the lists and mutually consent to the introduction of as many of the documents as possible. This will save a tremendous amount of trial time in formal proof, and save the delivery of notices to admit, etc. It is the sort of conduct that is expected of competent counsel by most trial judges and is greatly appreciated by the court.

Let us take a simple example, say an action for specific performance in the sale of a house in which you act for the vendor. There are only two issues:

(1) the validity of a requisition on title, and
(2) damages.

You could conveniently agree on two document briefs — the one dealing with the contract and its performance and the other with damages. By agreement the first brief could contain an index, the agreement of purchase and sale and copies of the letters passing between the solicitors dealing with requisitions on title. The second could contain an index and summary of the claim, together with back-up documents that establish the claim, such as the subsequent agreement of purchase and sale, statement of adjustments, tax bills, etc.

In preparation for trial, for your assistance at trial and the assistance of the trial judge, you should prepare a chronology. The chronology should have four columns: the left-hand column for the date, a column for your code numbers, exhibit numbers, etc., and then a wider column for the document or event. There should be plenty of space for the document or event and further space left in the fourth column so that the trial judge may add his own notes as the evidence is adduced.

It does not matter that the chronology is a number of pages long. Sometimes it is convenient to divide it into yearly and even monthly intervals with the year at the top of the page.

Following is a simple chronology which might be prepared by counsel for the plaintiff in an action by a vendor for breach of an agreement of purchase and sale.

Date	No.	Document or event	Remarks
Dec. 15/83	5	Agt. of purch. and sale – $195,000	
Dec. 28/83	12	Ltr solr for purchsr to solr for vdr	
Jan. 4/84	14	Stat. Decln re use	
Jan. 5/84	18	Ltr solr for vdr to slr for purchsr	

Date	No.	Document or event	Remarks
Jan. 7/84	21	Ltr solr for purchsr to solr for vdr	
Jan. 11/84	24	Ltr solr for vdr to solr for purchsr	
Jan. 15/84		Closing date	
Jan. 15/84	29, 30, 31, 32	Tender	
Feb. 1/84		Property re-listed	
Feb. 15/84		Property resold	
Mar. 12/84		Resale closed	

The trial book

You should always have a trial book for your own use. This is sometimes called a brief. However, I use the term "brief" to mean a binder of documents dealing with a particular subject, such as damages. In a complicated case you may have a number of different briefs. The trial book will need an index and probably tabbed dividers by subject matter. It should contain the following as a minimum:

(1) pleadings;
(2) copies of any affidavits that have been filed dealing with the facts, for example, affidavits filed on a motion for an interim injunction (the original affidavits should be kept apart because you may need to use the originals in cross-examination);
(3) your analysis of the case and the issues;
(4) your chronology;

(5) notes for your opening statement;

(6) the statements or proof of witnesses — if there is no statement you need a memorandum of the evidence of the witness;

(7) notes for your cross-examination of each witness that you anticipate being called against you;

(8) copies of the main documents;

(9) your master index of documents.

Some counsel prefer to keep their trial notes in a separate book. This is quite satisfactory.

You will need a separate brief of law including statutes, regulations, texts and cases all properly indexed, paginated and tabbed.

Be sure that you have your brief with you. It sounds trite, but I will tell you an absolutely true story to illustrate the point. A leading counsel, formerly a judge of the Supreme Court of Canada, was retained to take an appeal in that court. He stayed overnight at the Chateau Laurier and in checking out put down his brief case. Having checked out he picked up what he thought was his brief case and walked the short distance to the courthouse. Fortunately, he was for the respondent because when he opened the brief case in court he found it full of samples of ladies' underwear! His junior was able to exchange brief cases with the irate ladies' wear salesman back at the hotel before the respondent was called on.

If there is going to be an argument on admissibility of evidence, you may wish to prepare a brief of law for the argument.

In an injury case you will need a damage brief. It is usually unnecessary to include all the hospital records. Only include the important records, such as reports on operative procedures and discharge summaries. Again, this brief must be all properly indexed, paginated and tabbed.

Examinations for discovery and any other transcribed oral evidence should be summarized and indexed by subject matter. You may wish to include the subject matter index in your trial book.

Your trial briefs should be appropriately labelled and may have binders of different colours. For example, blue for law, red for damages.

It all sounds like a lot of trouble, and of course it is, but it is all worth while in the long run. In a substantial case two counsel are usually required. The prime jobs of the junior will be to note the evidence and to look after the paper.

Help the judge

The judge should have a copy of every document produced in evidence for his or her own use. It is impossible for a judge to follow the examination of a witness on a document without a copy. The judge will want to underline and note up his or her copy.

The documents going in on consent should be placed in a book or books, properly indexed and marked as an exhibit, *with a copy for the judge.* No doubt further documents will have to be marked, and the judge should be provided with a series of hard cover, loose-leaf binders complete with numbered spacers so that, as fresh documents are filed, the judge's copy can be punched and inserted in his or her book. In this way, for example, when a witness is referred to exhibit number 156, the judge can quickly turn to his or her own copy.

In long complicated cases most judges prepare a summary

of the evidence and exhibits after court. It is helpful if the judge can take a copy of the exhibits to his or her chambers for this purpose and avoid the necessity of the court registrar carting the original documents back and forth.

A copy of your book or books of authorities should be handed to the judge as early as possible, preferably during the opening or, if you are for the defence, immediately thereafter.

The judge will want to read the authorities to help him or her understand the issues, and so be better able to follow the thrust of the evidence. Again, the judge can underline pertinent parts of the authorities. If you anticipate an oral judgment you can also anticipate that the judge will quote from the authorities you have provided and which he or she has had an opportunity of reading well ahead of the argument. What a change from the old days when counsel brought trolley loads of books into the court room and the judge could estimate the length of the argument by the number of books lined up on counsel's desk! It was then considered rather bad form to try to read the citations of opposing counsel. Now it is considered good form to exchange books of authorities relied on before the trial.

CHAPTER 19

OPENING

Opening generally

IT IS PERFECTLY natural to be nervous, particularly before the start of a trial. I think that all good counsel get the adrenalin going before and during a trial, and this was one of the reasons I enjoyed counsel work. It was so exciting. Now that I am on the Bench I can be more relaxed.

However, it is sometimes difficult for young counsel who wonders before the judge comes in why in Heaven he or she spent seven years in university and law school just to be exposed to this torture. I remember my first appeal. My opponent was a delightful gentleman who shortly afterwards went to the Court of Appeal himself. He came over and asked me if I was nervous, and when I told him I was he said: "So am I, and let me tell you that when you stop being nervous you won't be any good as counsel."

Long before the trial you as counsel have given careful thought to the theory of the case. What really are the issues and how are you going to prove the essential facts to establish your case? You have to present your theory of the case in the opening and hold to this theory throughout the trial. You can plead in the alternative but you can hardly present facts in the alternative. For example, in a contract case it might be acceptable to deny that a contract was executed and plead in the

109

alternative that if it was, its execution was obtained by undue influence. This would be no good at a trial.

Opening is usually one of the least well done parts of a trial and its importance is generally under-estimated. In England, the opening is often left to junior counsel. In my opinion, this should never be done. Lawsuits are, to a great extent, contests between counsel. The opening address is counsel's opportunity not only to tell the court about the case but also to impress his or her personality on the court. A good counsel should be able to dominate the court room, and with the opening you have the opportunity of telling the court the story, without interruption, in such a way that judgment for your client appears inevitable.

First impressions of a case often last. Juries often make up their minds quickly. This is the first and, particularly with a jury, possibly the most important step in the process of persuasion. Some studies in the United States have shown that the jurors' ultimate decision corresponds with their tentative opinion after the opening statement in over 80 per cent of the cases.

As with any aspect of the trial, opening needs preparation. Some counsel write out their opening address and read it to the court. In my opinion, this should not be done: it tends to be monotonous and boring. There is a loss of spontaneity. Particularly with a jury it is necessary to maintain "eye contact". It is better to work from note headings. Take your proper position in the court room (see Chapter 9) and stay there except to introduce exhibits.

An opening is a simple, well-told narrative of the facts in chronological order without argument. It should not be excessively detailed. Do not go over the evidence of each witness you intend to call in order, because to do so becomes boring and also takes away the interest of the judge and jury when the witnesses are called. With an over-detailed opening the court already knows what the witness is going to say. There is no sense of anticipation and there may perhaps be a sense of hearing something that has been rehearsed.

You must never express a personal opinion. You are an advocate and it is not your opinion that matters. If you should express a personal opinion the judge may well interrupt, and there is nothing much worse for your opening, particularly with a jury. This does not mean that you should be neutral or without any emotion in the conduct of a trial. Your sincerity and belief in the rightness of your case should be clear to everyone.

Counsel will often be diffident in their opening. For example, counsel will say "I expect to be able to show that . . ." or "I anticipate that . . .". I think this is a mistake. Whenever possible you should be positive in your statements of fact. For example, you could say:

> My client, Mr. Smith, was driving north on Spadina Road in the City of Toronto at a reasonable rate of speed and as his car entered the intersection of Burton Road, after stopping to permit east-west traffic to clear, it was struck on the left side by the car owned and driven by Mr. Brown, the defendant.

Be careful, however, not to overstate your case. It is generally better to understate than to overstate. If your evidence does not live up to part of your opening then the court, and particularly a jury, may doubt your whole case and possibly your own integrity.

It is a mistake to try to be humorous in a trial, particularly in the opening. A sense of humour is important to counsel, and occasionally during a trial something amusing will be said and this helps to break the tension; but a forced attempt at humour usually falls flat and, in any event, the opening is no place for it.

The opening is not for argument. You have nothing to argue about yet. Your recital of the facts is argument enough at this stage of the trial.

Do not anticipate the defence; this only throws doubt on your case and lends substance to the defence.

The opening should only be as long as the complexity of the case requires. Be neat, chronological, logical and brief.

To open properly you must thoroughly understand the case and isolate the issues. In many trials there is only one issue; in complicated trials there may be two or three or possibly more. After you have "told the story" it is well to point up the issues. For example:

> There are only two issues in this case:
> 1. Did Mr. Smith sign the will in the presence of two witnesses who also signed? and
> 2. Did he have the mental capacity to make a will at that time?

Opening to a judge alone

As my co-author said in Chapter 10, in courts where counsel slips are in use there is no need to give your name. You start by introducing opposing counsel:

> May it please Your Lordship (or Your Ladyship), I appear for the plaintiff. My friend, Peter Brown, appears for the defendant.

In a simple case only a short opening is necessary. Most judges read the record before coming into court, and if the issues appear to be simple they may try to speed up the proceedings by saying that they have read the record, with the implication that little, if any, opening address is necessary. Records only give part of the story and are often wrong. Do not be intimidated. It is still necessary to outline the issues and introduce certain documents.

In a civil action that has been properly prepared with an adequate pre-trial conference and with the necessary exchange of documents and reports, counsel should be able to agree on most of the exhibits. These exhibits should be bound together, properly indexed and paginated and marked during the opening as a consent exhibit book or books with a copy for each counsel and the judge.

It must be made clear to the court that these documents that are in the exhibit book are going in as exhibits. That is, if the documents are copies, the documents on consent are to be treated as true copies of the originals. Letters that are addressed are admitted to have been sent in the usual course of business and received by the addressee, so that no further proof of these documents is required.

Now is the time to hand over a chronology for the judge and opposing counsel (see Chapter 18). The chronology is handed to the judge on the basis that the contents will be proved as the trial progresses. You should not include any disputed matter in the chronology. You should warn the judge of any legal issues that may arise during the course of the trial: usually questions of admissibility but also, for example, the ability of a young witness to take the oath. You should hand up and exchange your authorities on these issues. This is the time to introduce your surveys and photographs and, if it is a products liability case, the defective product. The mouse in the bottle for example. These items should go in on consent, but if there is no consent then with a judge alone they should go in subject to further proof.

Talking of the "mouse in the bottle" reminds me to impress on you the absolute necessity of carefully preserving this type of exhibit. I once defended a case involving a bottle of ginger ale that allegedly exploded badly cutting a woman's legs. The plaintiff alleged that the bottle had exploded, while the defence theory was that the woman had dropped the bottle which had shattered. The question to be answered was: was it pressure from inside or the application of force from outside that shattered the bottle? Only an expert could give the answer. Counsel for the plaintiff, who was very difficult, had the broken bottle and refused to turn it over for examination. I duly obtained an order for its production and finally the fragments were turned over to me all neatly tied up in a blue Birks' box. I left the box on the corner of my desk that night but next morning it was gone. A frantic call to the building manager finally produced the cleaning woman who had looked inside the box, seen the broken fragments of the bottle and thrown it all out. So ended the case.

Do not try to introduce such items with a jury in opening unless they are going in on consent. In a technical case, and I include in this a medical malpractice action, you should prepare a glossary of technical terms for the judge, the court reporter and your opponent. Now is the time to hand it in.

Opening to a jury

Much of what has already been said applies to a jury

opening, but a jury opening is of much greater importance than an opening to a judge alone. The process is new to the jury and your opening will have to be longer. If the judge has not already done so you will want to tell the jury a little about the mechanics of the trial.

After the formal introduction, which includes "members of the jury", you speak to the jury and not to the judge. Introduce your client as well as counsel:

> May it please Your Lordship (or Your Ladyship) and members of the jury, my name is John Smith. I appear for the plaintiff, Robert Burn. My friend, Peter Jones, appears for the defendant.

You want to get the jury to identify with your client. The counsel table is reserved for counsel except with permission of the judge. Now is an appropriate time to ask the judge's permission for your client to come up from the body of the court and sit at the counsel table. This will permit the jury to identify your client.

I acted for the plaintiff in my first Supreme Court jury trial. The defendant was a motorist who was uninsured. Defence counsel was a Q.C. who later became a good friend. He had his law clerk sit beside him at the counsel table and did not introduce him to the court. I was lucky enough to win and afterwards spoke to one of the jurors, a practice which was then followed. He told me that the jury knew the defendant was insured because defence counsel had the insurance adjuster sitting beside him all through the trial!

As in any newspaper story you give the headlines first:

> This is a case about a young woman who was crossing

Yonge Street in Toronto in a pedestrian cross-walk at mid-day when she was knocked down by a car and seriously injured.

or

This case involves serious injury caused to my client, Betty Smith, by a bottle of soda water that exploded showering her with glass fragments.

You must be careful not to mention any evidence that might be ruled inadmissible because, if you do, this may lead to a mistrial and a penalty in costs. You should clear any exhibits such as photographs and plans before showing them to the jury. This means that you should get the consent of opposing counsel to the items being marked as exhibits, or speak to the trial judge in the presence of opposing counsel about the matter before the case starts to get permission to show them to the jury during the opening.

The judge has probably told the jury already that nothing said to them in opening is evidence but, if not, it may be well to tell them, so that when they are told this later it will not detract from your opening.

You have to give the jury an outline of the case so that the jurors can better understand the evidence. The evidence may go in in rather a disjointed way, and unless the jury have an over-all appreciation of the case it will be difficult to follow. Never talk down to a jury. Use simple everyday English that will be easily understood. Be moderate and speak with sincerity but without excess emotion.

If your case has a problem area, known to the defence, it may be well to defuse the problem not only in your examination in chief but also in your opening. For example, if your client is an illegal immigrant who has been injured bring it out in your opening statement rather than having this fact extracted for the first time in cross-examination: you appear to be frank, with nothing to conceal.

If you are opening an injury case you should discuss the injury and the effect of the injury on your client in some detail. You must not tell the jury the figures you are claiming but there is much to be gained by telling them of the injury, supporting the opening by the evidence and reviewing the injury again in closing.

Opening a criminal case is to some extent different in that Crown counsel should be, and should be seen to be, impartial. He is still an advocate, but it is his job to bring out all the relevant evidence in a fair way and the opening should be a fair statement of the relevant facts.

Opening the defence

You have the right to open the defence if you are going to adduce evidence. This is seldom necessary in a non-jury case because the issues have probably been clearly defined by the plaintiff's evidence and your cross-examination. You should nearly always open your defence with a jury. You have usually pointed the way in your cross-examination but you still need to give the jury the defence theory. What inferences should the jury draw from the proved facts? What is the defence theory of the injury? You also need to introduce any counterclaim.

Opening the defence is different from opening the case because it is part reply and part opening. If the plaintiff's case has fallen below the opening, now is the time to draw it to the jury's attention.

For example:

> Mr. White, for the plaintiff, in his opening address said that the plaintiff was driving his car north on Spadina Road and stopped at the intersection of Burton for some time to permit east-west traffic to clear. You will remember that the evidence that was adduced on behalf of the plaintiff showed exactly the opposite: that is, that his car did not stop before entering the intersection but drove right into the intersection when it was struck by that driven by Mr. Brown, my client.

You should keep your defence opening as short as possible. The jury already know a lot about the case and all you need to do is to put the defence position clearly to them.

CHAPTER 20

EXAMINATION IN CHIEF

General

EXAMINATION IN CHIEF is a set piece. All must be planned and the questions and answers rolled forward in careful chronological order. There is no thrust and parry here — that is for the cross-examiner.

You must present the evidence in a complete and convincing form and in order to do this you must get each witness to tell the whole story, usually chronologically, without prompting, apparently honestly, with spontaneity and, if possible, without interruption.

In most cases there are only a few important points and you should restrict your examination to these points so far as possible. With the backlog of cases the trial judge will appreciate a determined resolve to try cases quickly. So present your evidence with dispatch, keep the proceedings lively and get on with your case.

Organizing the witnesses

Long before the trial you will have carefully considered the issues in the case and if you are acting for the plaintiff you will have noted the essential matters to be covered in order to succeed. You must now decide who will be called as witnesses to cover these points and what areas can be covered by reading in from the examination for discovery and from documents.

There is no property in a witness and you are permitted to interview any witness before trial. You must do this in order to prepare each witness for trial and to assess the quality of each witness. Remember that, as counsel, with some exceptions, you to a great extent vouch for each witness that you put in the witness box.

The witnesses should be interviewed individually. In a motor vehicle case, for example, if you interview the witnesses together there is a tendency for them to give exactly the same estimates of time, speed and distance with the result that the evidence sounds rehearsed.

Go over the evidence of each witness in the order that you will examine him or her at trial. If there are inconsistencies in the evidence point them out to the witness and seek his or her explanation.

It is essential to assess the witness. Is he or she intelligent, verbose, argumentative or biased? Remember, every witness that you call is dangerous to your cause and may destroy your case in cross-examination. There is a tendency of many counsel to call unnecessary witnesses.

If you have two strong witnesses to prove that the traffic signal was green for your client, why call a third who might waver on the point or, even worse, in cross-examination?

It is only after you have interviewed each witness that you will decide which of them will be called and in what order.

Witnesses may well be excluded, and in addition to interviewing the witnesses it is sometimes advisable to arrange for one or more actually to go to the court house and see a trial in progress so that the procedure will seem less strange when they are called to the witness box.

In certain types of cases, for example where credibility is an issue, and if your witnesses are well prepared, it is advisable to ask for an order excluding witnesses, other than the parties and the experts, from the court room for the duration of the trial. Such an order may adversely affect the witnesses of your less well prepared opponent and will lead to greater spontaneity in the evidence.

In interviewing the witnesses, bear in mind that, generally speaking, only experts can give opinion evidence but any qualified person may give an opinion based on common experience. For example, most adults can give an opinion on the sobriety of another.

You must prepare your witnesses for cross-examination. Cross-examine them a bit yourself and warn them to tell the truth whatever happens. This sounds trite but it is necessary. For example, in cross-examination some counsel will ask the witness whether he has discussed his evidence with his lawyer before trial. A witness may think that this is improper and will deny the suggestion — an obvious untruth. If he has been told to tell the truth he will admit the pre-trial interview and perhaps have the opportunity to add that he was told by his lawyer to tell truthfully exactly what happened. Also tell the witness simply to answer the questions and not try to guess ahead — that is, to guess the purpose of the cross-examiner. In my experience, many witnesses have this fault of guessing ahead. It tends to show the bias of the witness, is frustrating to counsel and annoying to the trial judge. For example, on cross-examination, a witness is asked whether the driver of a car was staggering after the accident. The witness will think to himself, "the lawyer is trying to get me to say that he was drunk" and will answer "he was not drunk" which, of course, is not responsive. So warn your witnesses simply to answer the questions asked and not try to out-think or outsmart the other lawyer.

Explain to the witnesses that everything they say must be taken down by the court reporter and that, in addition, the judge will want to take complete notes of the evidence. As a result, they must speak clearly, in a loud voice and relatively slowly. They must answer the questions, not nod or say "uh-huh".

Do not coach the witnesses. It is alright to point out inconsistencies or improbabilities, but they should be urged to tell their story in a natural, unrehearsed way.

People act on hearsay, and the evidentiary rule excluding hearsay evidence has been much criticized and, to some extent, relaxed. However, in preparing your witnesses for trial you must warn them about the rule. You will look foolish if you have to try to explain the rule to a witness in the middle of his evidence, and the judge will think you are poorly prepared.

Tell your witnesses how to address the judge. I am sure that I have been called many names during my time on the Bench. Among others I have been called "Your Excellency" and "My God".

One of my first murder trials as a judge was in a small town in northern Ontario. Everything had gone wrong — the jury should have acquitted after five minutes but was still out after five hours and I think they just wanted a free dinner. The hotel was uncomfortable and the weather inclement. The sheriff was sloppy and kept tripping over his sword and losing his cocked hat and, in addition, insisted on calling me "Your Honour", which was not good for the pride of a newly appointed Supreme Court Judge. When he told me that the jury had a verdict I told him not to call me "Your Honour", to which he replied, "Very well, Your Excellency". That put me in my place!

During a medical malpractice trial one of the defence counsel, who I think was rather annoyed with me, and was certainly annoyed at the answer of a witness, struck his forehead with the palm of his hand and said, "Oh My God". I assured him that "My Lord" was quite sufficient.

In the Supreme Court with a sophisticated witness "My Lord" is satisfactory and in the county or district court "Your Honour", but these forms of address may sound unreal to less sophisticated witnesses, and I suggest that you tell such witnesses to address the judge simply as "Sir" or "Madam".

Watch out for the drunk. I remember a witness who appeared rather jolly in the morning. Unfortunately his evidence was not finished by the lunch break and by 2.30 he was pretty well gone. About 3 o'clock he fell out of the witness box on his head, cutting himself rather badly. Fortunately a doctor was the next witness up and was in court so that the injured witness was quickly patched up and carted off to hospital.

Some counsel have themselves video-taped giving a talk to a prospective witness and have the witnesses see the video tape before the trial. This may well help but nothing takes the place of the personal interview. The purpose of the interview is not only to instruct the witness but also, and perhaps more importantly, to help you judge the strength or weakness of the witness.

Try to keep your witnesses reasonably happy. Too many people who see an accident fail to give their name to the police, and no wonder in view of the way so many witnesses are treated in our courts. So treat your witnesses with consideration. Tell them, if necessary, how they should dress when they come to court — "Dress as if you were going to church" — so that they will not be embarrassed. The way your witnesses are presented reflects on you as counsel. See that their loss of time is kept to a minimum and that they suffer no loss of income so that all in all, after they leave the court room, they feel pleased to have helped in the administration of justice.

Order of calling witnesses

Generally you should call your plaintiff or defendant first. However, there are exceptions where you may wish to call some preliminary witness or witnesses to set the scene. For example, in a motor vehicle accident case you may wish to call a surveyor, prove aerial photographs and photographs of the scene before the plaintiff is put in the box.

If witnesses other than the parties have been excluded and you are not calling the plaintiff first you should, except with leave of the court, exclude the plaintiff from the court room while these other witnesses testify. Remember you wish to present the evidence in an orderly way, and chronologically if possible, so you should call all the witnesses dealing with one aspect of the litigation in order. For example, in a medical malpractice action you might have three groups: (a) witnesses dealing with the facts of the alleged malpractice; (b) expert witnesses who will give their opinion on the facts; and (c) witnesses who will deal with damages.

Try to start with a strong witness on any aspect of the case. This witness will bear the brunt of the cross-examination. Then put in your weaker or less important witnesses and try to end with a good one.

Remember you are not allowed to split your case, that is, just call some of your witnesses to prove a *prima facie* case and then try to call the rest of the witnesses in reply. This is not only unfair, since the defendant is entitled to know the case he has to meet, but it is also not permitted.[1]

You are permitted to read in from the examination for discovery of the opposite party as part of your case. Inexperienced counsel often fall into grave trouble in this area for two reasons:

(1) You can be forced to read in all relevant evidence on the topic once you have started; and

(2) the evidence that you read in goes in as part of your case.

If you are not careful you can destroy your own case by reading in from discovery. If there is no evidence to challenge the evidence that has been read in then it will be accepted unless inherently improbable. It is, however, still open to the party to call evidence to show that the answers on discovery should not be believed. But why set up part of the other side's case in order to have to knock it down?[2]

If you have made the mistake of reading in too much the court still has power to permit you to withdraw the evidence.[3]

Trial book

As stated in Chapter 18, you should have a loose-leaf trial book. It will contain a number of tabbed divisions, and in one of these divisions there will be your notes or "proof" for each

---

[1]*Allcock, Laight & Westwood Ltd. v. Patton et al.*, [1967] 1 O.R. 18.
[2]See *Clark v. McCrohan*, [1948] O.W.N. 172, [1948] 2 D.L.R. 283 (C.A.); *Reti et al. v. Fox et al.* (1976), 2 C.P.C. 62 (Ont. C.A.).
[3]*Kirkby v. Booth*, [1964] 1 O.R. 286, 42 D.L.R. (2d) 32 (H.C.J.).

witness that you intend to call and quite often a copy of that witness's signed statement. The trial book is dealt with in greater detail in Chapter 18.

Either during or immediately after your interview with the witness you should dictate a detailed note of his evidence, send him a copy and ask him to make any corrections or additions. As an alternative, you can send your witness home and ask him to write out a detailed note of everything that occurred that has anything to do with the case and send you a copy. This note of evidence will go in your trial book and will be your guide for your examination in chief.

With the exception of hypothetical questions, and questions in difficult technical cases, do not write out the questions you intend to ask. Take your position in the court room with your trial book handy, face the witness and gently take him through his evidence. Occasionally you can glance down at your notes to ensure that all of the points have been covered.

The court's attention should be centred on the witness, not on counsel, so stay still except to produce exhibits.

Your paper work must be in good order so that there is no fumbling for exhibit numbers. Your exhibit lists, production lists and chronology will help and should be kept at hand for easy reference (see Chapter 18).

The examination

You must first introduce the witness to the court and put the witness at ease. Here you can and should lead. It is unnecessary to ask his or her name — that was given when he or she was sworn. Address the witness as Mr., Mrs., or Miss. Do not address a witness, other than a child, by his or her first name: it is quite out of keeping with the seriousness of the occasion. Do not be familiar or flippant. Ask a few simple questions about the witness's background. Then show how his or her evidence is relevant, for example:

> Q. Mr. Smith, I understand that you witnessed an accident that occurred at the intersection of Bay and Bloor Streets in the City of Toronto on September 5th, 1982?

Note that in this question the witness is referred to the fact, not just the date. People remember facts, not dates, and a reference to the date alone may cause confusion. An honest witness who is asked:

> Q. Did you witness an accident on September 5th, 1982?

may well answer that he does not know, since he cannot remember the date and has witnessed several accidents.

A further example of a proper introductory question is:

> Q. At my request did you examine a section of pipe which I now show to you and which has been marked as exhibit 32 at this trial?

Then proceed through the witness's evidence in chronological order relatively slowly so that the judge can make a clear note of the evidence. You proceed calmly, deliberately and clearly. Try to avoid interruptions by your opponent, so do not go beyond the bounds of leading. Maintain your dominion over the witness but prompt the witness to bring out the evidence in his or her own words and, if appropriate, in his or her own way. Do not ask the same question twice — you may get a different answer.

Exhaust all the points at every stage in the evidence before moving on.

It sounds trite but only ask one question at a time. Some counsel ask two or three. For example:

Q. What happened then? So tell me in your own words what he said. Or did he say anything then?

It sounds ridiculous but this sort of question is asked all the time. The witness just gets confused and the judge has to come to the rescue.

Do not show irritation with your own witness. You must be patient.

When a document is tendered as an exhibit you should give a description. It is for the judge to accept the exhibit. For example, after having the witness identify his or her signature on a deed, it would be improper for counsel to say "That is exhibit 6". The proper thing is to say, "May that be exhibit 6, My Lord — deed from John Jones to Henry Smith dated June 6th, 1982 and registered on June 8th, 1982?" This helps the judge in his notes and list of exhibits and helps the registrar who must also list and describe the exhibits. Remember, the judge must rule on the admissibility of each exhibit before it is marked.

In examination in chief and throughout the trial use simple language. Everyone knows that you are a lawyer and there is no need to try to prove it by your language. Even the words "plaintiff" and "defendant" are misunderstood and get mixed up by some witnesses, so do not use these terms. The simpler the language the better. For example, do not say, "Prior to that occasion had you ever met the defendant?" Rather, "Had you ever met Mr. Smith, the driver of the red Ford, before?"

All counsel tend to develop habits of speech. Some are bad

and become annoying. It is particularly annoying to have counsel repeat the answer given by the witness.

There are usually some weak points in your case. For example, in a criminal defence your client may have a criminal record. Under the law as it stands today he may be cross-examined on his record, so if you call him, and the other counsel knows of the record, bring it out in chief: get rid of the sting of it.

> Q. Mr. Smith, I understand that you were convicted of theft in 1973 when you were only nineteen years old?
> A. Yes, Sir.
> Q. You received a suspended sentence?
> A. Yes.

Many witnesses, in preparation for trial and to assist their memory, make notes to help them without telling counsel. Once in the witness box out come the notes. This should not happen with a well-briefed witness, but if it does, tell the witness to put the notes away.

A witness may refresh his memory by looking at notes made by him contemporaneously, or made by others and adopted by him at the time.[4] Moreover, it is not even necessary that the witness have an independent recollection of the fact.[5]

The notes do not become evidence but must be produced, may be cross-examined upon and may at the instance of the opposite counsel be marked as an exhibit.[6]

It is often necessary to examine a witness by using an interpreter. You must, if possible, obtain an interpreter with

---

[4]*Daynes v. B.C. Electric R. Co.* (1912), 7 D.L.R. 767 (B.C.C.A.), affd on this point 19 D.L.R. 266 (S.C.C.).

[5]*Fleming v. Toronto R.W. Co.* (1911), 25 O.L.R. 317 (C.A.).

[6]*Senat v. Senat*, [1965] 2 All E.R. 505, [1965] P. 172.

experience. Do not settle for a relative or a friend. Interview the interpreter before he is called and make sure that he understands his function, which is not simply to interpret but also to stop the witness by hand signals in a long answer so that the interpreter can keep up and so that the interpretation is accurate. There is nothing much more ridiculous than a long answer with the interpreter obviously forgetting half of it. The interpreter should never ask the witness a question himself and, of course, must use the first person. As usual, you address the witness directly. For example:

    Q. Where do you live?

is correct.

    Q. Mr. Interpreter, ask the witness where he lives.

is wrong.

Try as far as possible to look at the witness and try to forget the presence of the interpreter.

When you have finished your examination, sit down. Although some counsel disagree with me, I suggest that you do not go over to your senior, junior or client and ask what you have forgotten. It shows weakness; and above all, do not say, as so many counsel do:

    Q. Is there anything else that you would like to tell us?

Leading questions

A leading question is a question that suggests an answer, or that assumes certain facts not yet attested to by the witness. For example, where there has been no description by the witness of the clothing worn by the accused:

Q. He was wearing shorts, wasn't he?

or even worse:

Q. Were the shorts that he was wearing white?

The general rule is that you should not lead in examination in chief. Quite apart from the rule, an answer obtained to a leading question does not have the same strength as an answer given to a non-leading question.

There are, however, a number of exceptions to the rule:

1. It is quite proper, and to be preferred, that you lead on introductory and undisputed matters.
2. After repeatedly trying to get a witness to deal with a point that he has forgotten, it is permissible to remind him of the point by a leading question.[7]
3. You may lead to put to a witness what a prior witness has said so that the witness can contradict this prior testimony.[8]
4. In accordance with the relevant *Evidence Act* you may cross-examine a witness who proves adverse on a prior inconsistent statement. The relevant section of the Act (*Canada Evidence Act* in criminal matters, provincial *Evidence Act* in civil matters) must be looked at carefully because there are substantial differences in the legislation.
5. It is normal and not objectionable to lead in the introduction of documents. For example:

Q. I show you a deed dated July 5th, 1982, between John Jones as grantor and Peter Smith as grantee. Does your signature appear on page 5 of the deed?

---

[7]*Maves v. G.T.P. Railway Co.* (1913), 5 W.W.R. 212 (Alta. C.A.).
[8]*Ibid.*

Examination of experts

What I have already said about examination in chief also applies to expert witnesses. There are, however, certain additional matters that need to be considered. Each expert will have prepared a report. Many jurisdictions require that the reports be exchanged before trial, and the new Ontario Rules so provide. The report should include the expert's *curriculum vitae* as an Appendix. It should deal with the facts, in chronological order, upon which the opinion is based and should state the expert's opinion.

An expert usually gives an opinion based, in part, on hearsay evidence. Before calling your expert you must be sure that you have already proved the factual basis for the opinion. Remember that the opinion is only as good as the facts upon which it is based.

You will need to put hypothetical questions to the witness. Your hypothetical question or questions must be accurate. To be sure, write the question out and go over it with the expert before trial.

The expert witness needs a special introduction. You must first establish his expertise. It is usual to produce the witness's c.v. and have it marked as an exhibit. Be sure that you have a copy for opposing counsel and the judge, but that is not enough. Particularly with a jury, it is necessary to take the witness through his qualifications.

Opposing counsel has the right to challenge, by way of cross-examination, the qualifications of a witness to give opinion evidence before the opinion evidence is received,[9] but this is not often done.

---

[9] *Baker v. Hutchinson et al.* (1976), 13 O.R. (2d) 591, 1 C.P.C. 291 (C.A.).

Having qualified the witness, it is most helpful in a non-jury trial to produce the expert's report and have it marked as an exhibit. The Ontario Court of Appeal, *per* Brooke J.A. in *Ferraro v. Lee*,[10] held that, on the wording of the relevant section of the Ontario *Evidence Act* a party cannot both mark a medical report and call the doctor who prepared the report. In practice, however, except in jury cases, this case is circumvented. The medical reports are exchanged and marked as exhibits on consent even though the reporting doctor is called as a witness.

The reports of experts other than doctors are also marked as exhibits on consent even though the expert is called to testify.

The expert's report is extremely helpful to the judge. The judge may be unfamiliar with some of the scientific terms and can better follow the evidence with the report in front of him or her without the necessity of making voluminous notes. After all, the object of the exercise is to make sure that the judge thoroughly understands the evidence and appreciates the opinion. Many judges will quote the reports in their reasons for judgment.

The report having been marked, all that is then needed is to take the expert step by step through the report to its conclusion.

10(1974), 2 O.R. (2d) 417, 43 D.L.R. (3d) 161 (C.A.).

CHAPTER 21

CROSS-EXAMINATION

A VERY FEW COUNSEL have a God-given talent, possibly a supreme understanding of people, that enables them to cross-examine without appearing to follow any particular pattern, ignoring all the usual rules, and still not put a foot wrong. But this is for the very few. Any counsel can learn to cross-examine adequately if he follows the rules.

The purpose of cross-examination is, first, to weaken or discredit the testimony of the witness given in chief and, second, to elicit those parts of the witness's evidence favourable to your case.

You will try to show the witness to be unworthy of credit by reason of inconsistent statements, inconsistency with proven facts, faulty memory, lack of opportunity to see or hear and the inherent improbability of his evidence.

You must tailor your cross-examination to the witness. Your manner in the cross-examination of a young girl will be quite different from that in your cross-examination of an experienced police officer. If a witness is belligerent you will cross-examine to show his bias. Generally speaking, you will be courteous to the witness. You will not bully or be sarcastic. There is a fine line that you must tread. If you go over the line and badger the witness, or are unfair in your cross-examination in any way, the judge and jury will become sympathetic and protective towards the witness. It is seldom necessary for counsel to interrupt in an attempt to protect the witness from the cross-examiner. If the cross-examination goes too far, or if the witness is being bullied, the judge will usually interrupt to protect the witness and this, of course, is much more effective, particularly with a jury.

The worst type of so-called cross-examination is the tedious review, in a loud voice, of the evidence of the witness given in chief in the vain hope that he will change his testimony. Those parts of the evidence that were vague are now clear. The ambiguities vanish. The judge and jury have the opportunity of hearing everything for the second time and the evidence is reinforced.

Do not cross-examine on a favourable answer. There is the danger that the witness has realized his mistake and will explain away the answer. Treasure his favourable answer for cross-examination of other opponents' witnesses and final argument.

In most cases there are only a few essential points on which you should cross-examine. In long complicated cases it is probably well to cross-examine following the points you wish to cover in chronological order. This is not necessary in short cases. Most counsel cross-examine at too great a length.

Sometimes a dishonest witness will exaggerate. If you can build exaggeration upon exaggeration it will become obvious to the court and his credibility will be destroyed.

Now to the rules. In my opinion, there are three primary rules that are essential to any good cross-examination and a number of secondary rules that apply in some cases. Here is the list. Each rule is explained in greater detail in the following pages.

PRIMARY RULES
1. Prepare your cross-examination carefully.
2. Always lead. Ask "closed" questions; never ask an "open" question.
3. Make your point and switch to another or stop.

SECONDARY RULES
1. Try to start well and end well.
2. Use simple language with short questions.
3. Do not ask a question unless you have a very good idea of the answer.
4. Do not get into arguments with the witness: keep your temper.
5. Be aware of the value of the "surprise" question.
6. Do not "pass a witness".

Primary rule 1. Preparation

As in every other part of the trial, preparation is vital. Remember most cases are won or lost before you get into court.

Before the trial you will have a good idea of the witnesses that will be called against you. Prepare your cross-examination of each witness. Take a sheet of paper, put the witness's name at the top and make your notes. You will often have a good idea of what the witness will say in chief. Remember to look for:

(1) inconsistent statements;
(2) inconsistency with proven facts;
(3) faulty memory;
(4) lack of opportunity to see or hear.

You often have available a transcript of the evidence of the witness from examination for discovery, inquest, preliminary hearing, etc. All of the transcripts must be carefully read, summarized and indexed under subject headings to page and question numbers so that you can quickly pick up discrepancies in the evidence of the various witnesses called against you and also of the witness in the box. You will want to face the witness with both types of discrepancy. There is a set formula for putting prior evidence to a witness. You must first get the witness to confirm the evidence given in chief and then put the inconsistency to him. For example:

Q. Mr. Smith, you have just told us that although you did not sign as a witness you were present in the hospital room when Mrs. White signed her will in the presence of Dr. Brown and the nurse Rebecca Jones?

A. Yes.

Q. Was this evidence true?

A. Yes.

Q. Mr. Smith, do you remember being examined for discovery on oath in the office of Mr.   in Toronto on March 21st, 1981?

A. Yes.

Q. Mr. Smith, I am going to read to you certain questions and answers that you gave at that time and I am then going to ask you whether or not those questions were put to you, whether you gave those answers and whether or not the answers were true. Do you understand?

A. Yes.

Q. My Lord, may I refer you to page 20, questions 48 to 52?

Then read the questions and answers indicating that the witness was in the hospital corridor at the time of the signing.

Q. Were you asked those questions and did you give those answers?

By this time the witness will have realized the inconsistency and may try to hedge. You may have to threaten to call the reporter as a witness. The witness will probably finally admit to the questions and answers and that he was under oath. You then point out the inconsistency and, if you prefer the earlier answers, may well suggest that his memory in the prior proceeding would have been better since it was closer to the events described. Do not ask him to explain the inconsistency. He may come up with some fairly reasonable explanation. If he starts to explain try this:

> Mr. Smith, your counsel has the opportunity of re-examining and no doubt, if he considers it advisable, he will ask you to explain the inconsistency.

The sting of the inconsistency is left and opposing counsel may well be afraid to revive the issue in re-examination.

In a jury trial you must remember that if you intend to use the transcript of the examination for discovery in cross-examination you should first obtain the trial judge's permission to explain the process to the jury.

Do not forget to point out inconsistencies between the evidence of the witness in the box and that of a prior witness. For example:

> Q. Mr. Smith, you have told the court that you were in the hospital room at the time the will was signed. Is that right?
> A. Yes.
> Q. Dr. Brown, who signed as a witness to the will, has already testified that there were only three people present when the will was signed and you were not one of them. Which one of you is wrong?

The evidence given by the witness before or at trial may be

inconsistent with proven facts. You should have complete mastery of the facts and, if you do, these inconsistencies become evident and can be pointed out to the witness. Here there is no harm in asking for his explanation. He either cannot explain the inconsistency or blames the inconsistency on faulty memory. Either way you win.

You may cross-examine a witness on inconsistencies between his evidence and a prior written or oral statement. If you have a written statement from the witness you should not just show it to him: have him identify his signature and mark it as an exhibit. A statement should contain a wealth of personal information, such as age, marital status, children, residence, business, etc. The witness may claim that the statement was really the statement of the investigator, and you should start out by getting his confirmation of these personal facts that could only come from the witness. Then suggest that on a certain date he was visited by an investigator who asked him questions, noted the answers and had him sign the statement. At this point you have him identify his signature. The statement can then be marked as an exhibit, with a copy for the judge. Then read the statement to him, sentence by sentence, and have him confirm the truth of each sentence.

Human memory is faulty. It can be buttressed by notes made at the time of the happening of the events. You will know through proper preparation and production whether or not there are any notes. If there are not, you may wish to explore carefully the frailty of the witness's memory. For example, in a car accident case — you know the facts — you may wish to explore the colour, make, number of doors, etc., of the cars involved. Unless the witness owns one of the cars he will have forgotten these details and may start guessing.

If he is right on the first couple of answers switch away to something else.

In many cases the evidence of a witness depends on his ability to see or hear. Sometimes this can be attacked, particularly the ability to see. Sometimes it is helpful for counsel actually to visit the scene and have measurements taken by a law clerk or an investigator who can later be called to testify, if necessary, and also have photographs taken. In one murder trial the accused had put forward an alibi defence and testified that while having a shower in his apartment he heard the screams of the victim in the apartment below. A simple test with a policewoman screaming in the apartment below and a policeman in the shower above showed that this was impossible.

Sometimes the evidence of the witness is so improbable that it lacks credibility. By pointing out the improbability to the witness you highlight its improbability to the judge and jury.

By the time you have done your preparation for the cross-examination you will have a number of notes on your sheets of paper in your trial book. You will have noted the anticipated weak points in the evidence and the areas on which you intend to cross-examine.

This does not mean that the cross-examination should become mechanical. One of Canada's leading counsel, who only took the largest cases and who was always attended by a retinue of junior counsel, students and clerks, prepared his cross-examination so well that every question and possible answer was typed up with accompanying notes. It was quite an experience to witness the great man turn a page of his trial book just as all the juniors, students and clerks turned their pages in their copies of the trial book. Great preparation — but a certain lack of the appearance of spontaneity!

Primary rule 2. Ask "closed" questions

Always lead and ask "closed" questions. Never ask an "open" question. A closed question permits of only one answer. An open question permits the witness to explain or repeat his evidence in chief.

In cross-examination counsel must dominate the witness. Cross-examination is completely different from examination in chief where counsel gently prompts the witness to bring out his evidence. In cross-examination you must never let the witness get out of control. Do not let him wriggle out of his inconsistencies or explain his evidence if you can possibly help it. Do not let him get away with an answer that is not responsive to the question. Force him to answer the question. If necessary appeal to the judge for help.

For example, in the cross-examination of a bank manager concerning the trust character of funds on deposit in a customer's account, do not ask:

Q. Did you know that these funds were trust funds?

You will get the wrong answer every time. You should use closed questions — something like this:

Q. I understand you were the manager when Brown Brothers Construction account was opened?

You know he was from discovery and the answer has to be Yes.

A. Yes.
Q. I suppose you took certain financial information from an officer of that company when the account was opened?

Again, you should know this from discovery, and even if you do not it is a safe assumption that the manager or one of his assistants took this information when the file was opened.

A. Yes.

Q. Did he tell you that the company was in the construction business?

Again, you know the answer from discovery, from the production of documents and from the very name of the company itself.

A. Yes.

Q. Did he give you a list of the construction projects in which the company was engaged?

A. Yes.

Q. Was the Terrytown Plaza one of the projects?

A. Yes.

Q. You knew Brown Brothers Construction was the general contractor for that project?

A. Yes.

Q. As such, you must have known that the actual construction would be performed by sub-contractors?

A. Yes.

Q. I produce and show you a cheque from Terrytown Plaza Company to Brown Brothers Construction for $400,000. Was this cheque cashed at your branch?

A. Yes.

Q. My Lord, may this cancelled cheque be marked as exhibit 34? Cheque from Terrytown Plaza Company to Brown Brothers Construction for $400,000 dated September 1st, 1982.

His Lordship: Yes — exhibit 34.

Q. This, then, would have been a payment on account of the building contract?

A. Yes.

Q. This, then, would be a trust fund for the benefit of unpaid sub-contractors?

A. Yes.

This bit of cross-examination is taken from my memory of my cross-examination of a bank manager in a case that finally ended up in the Supreme Court of Canada. The trial judge, with whom I later sat on the Divisional Court, for some reason that I cannot remember had taken a dislike to my client, or to me, or to my case. The answer that I got, if left alone, won the case for me. To my fury, the trial judge leaned over to the witness after the answer and said something like this:

> His Lordship: Mr. Smith, surely what you really meant was that all funds deposited in a bank are held in trust for someone, usually the customer, and you knew nothing different in this case?

The judge, of course, got an affirmative answer. I said nothing and switched away to something else.

Fortunately, either the bank manager was not too bright or he was honest, because when sometime later I asked him the same line of questions I got the right answer again. This time the judge was furious. To my amazement he leaned back from the Bench, took out a packet of cigarettes, lit one, and started to smoke. I do not think he could have been conscious of what he had done. I thought of saying, "When your Lordship has finished smoking, may I continue?" but no one said a thing, which is just as well or I might have ended up cited for contempt.

Defence counsel tells the story but adds that the trial judge, after a moment or two, threw the lighted cigarette into the waste paper basket beside the Bench starting a small fire, but this I do not remember.

Primary rule 3. Make your point and change to another or stop

When you get the answer you want change the subject at

once or stop your cross-examination. Many cross-examinations are ruined by that one last unnecessary question. You hardly ever hear a cross-examination that is too short. Most are too long. Never ask that last question.

Secondary rule 1. Start well and end well

Most witnesses are strangers to the court room. They are naturally ill at ease. They have passed through examination in chief and now feel more confident and may even be starting to enjoy themselves. They have, however, been warned of cross-examination and may be somewhat fearful. Do not put them at their ease again unless you want to lead them gently down the garden path to some helpful admission.

You usually have a good point that you can make. For example, some contradiction between the evidence the witness has just given and his prior testimony. Put it to him at once. In the same way keep a good point for the end so that when you sit down the court's impression of the witness will tend to be unfavourable.

Secondary rule 2. Use simple language with short questions

As I said earlier in Chapter 20, forget the legalese. Everyone knows you are a lawyer. You do not have to prove it by the language you use. This is particularly important before a jury. Use good understandable English. Do not talk about "motor vehicles proceeding": cars are driven.

Please, no Latin. Do not say this document contains "*inter alia*". A jury will not understand the phrase and most judges will think you are pretentious. Very often I find that the younger the counsel the more pretentious the language.

Secondary rule 3. Do not ask a question unless you have a very good idea of the answer

Through your preparation, your knowledge of the facts and knowledge of the witness you should know what the answer will be to your question. Sometimes you do not. If you do not know the answer and you consider it really necessary to your case to get an answer, then do not take the risk of asking the question right out. You have to build up to the vital question little by little and stop if you get the wrong answer to any of your preliminary questions. It is only when you have a solid background of helpful answers that you can take the, by this time, minimal risk and ask the vital question. This needs careful advance planning and you should write out your questions ahead of time.

Secondary rule 4. Do not get into arguments with the witness: keep your temper

To argue with a witness brings you down to his level and is embarrassing to the court. You must control the witness and not let him argue. Force him to answer the questions, if possible, with a Yes or No answer. Do not let him explain. Always keep your temper. If you lose your temper you stop thinking rationally and you are lost. Very occasionally you may pretend to lose your temper, but even this is dangerous because you will appear to have lost control of yourself and this is an embarrassment to everyone. This does not mean to say that you should be icy cold in your approach. You need to show some emotion and a belief in the rightness of your cause.

Secondary rule 5. Be aware of the value of the surprise question

Occasionally you can slip in a surprise question, catch the witness off guard, and he will answer truthfully. Keep it in mind in your preparation. Sometimes it will come to mind while the witness is in the box.

Secondary rule 6. Do not "pass" a witness

By this I mean that it is your obligation to put to the witness in cross-examination any conversation or act involving the witness about which you intend to call evidence and about which he has not already testified in chief. It is not only necessary to do this because if you do not the judge may stop you from adducing the evidence yourself, but it is also helpful to your cause since you give the judge and jury some idea of the evidence that you will be calling and the character of your defence.

This rule stems from a statement by Lord Herschell in the House of Lords in *Brown v. Dunn*, where he said:[1]

> Now, my Lords, I cannot help saying that it seems to me to be absolutely essential to the proper conduct of a cause, where it is intended to suggest that a witness is not speaking the truth on a particular point, to direct his attention to the fact by some questions put in cross-examination showing that that imputation is intended to be made, and not to take his evidence and *pass it by* as a matter altogether unchallenged, and then, when it is impossible for him to explain, as perhaps he might have been able to do if such questions had been put to him, the circumstances which it is suggested indicate that the story he tells ought not to be believed, to argue that he is a

---

[1](1893), 6 R. 67 (H.L.) at pp. 70-1. See also *Peters v. Perras* (1909), 42 S.C.R. 244 at p. 245; *Hamburg Manufacturing Co. v. Webb* (1911), 23 O.L.R. 44 (Div. Ct.) at p. 45.

witness unworthy of credit. My Lords, I have always understood that if you intend to impeach a witness you are bound, whilst he is in the box, to give him an opportunity of making any explanation which is open to him; and, as it seems to me, that is not only a rule of professional practice in the conduct of a case, but is essential to fair play and fair dealing with witnesses.

(Emphasis added)

For example, your client has told you of a conversation with the witness about which you intend to question your client in chief. The witness has not been asked about this conversation by his counsel. You must put the conversation to him.

> Q. I am instructed that my client, John Jones, met with you at your office on Friday, November 13th, 1981, at about 4 o'clock in the afternoon when the question of an extension of the time for payment of the note was discussed. Is that right?

No matter what the answer, you must press on:

> Q. I am told that at that time you said that if my client paid $5,000 on account, which he did, no further payment would be required for one year. Is that true?

You have an obligation to face the witness with these questions, otherwise you will be unable to adduce this evidence in defence. In addition, you are getting the defence theory before the judge and jury. This is particularly important with a jury since the jury have not had the opportunity of reading the pleadings, and have not yet heard your defence opening and they do not know what your defence will be.

Cross-examining the expert witness

In cross-examining an expert you follow the same rules. However, there are some additional points to be made.

The preparation for the cross-examination of an expert is even more important and considerably more difficult. You need help. The expert will, of course, be superior to you in knowledge in his field. You usually have a copy of the opposing expert's report, and under the new Ontario Rules you will have. You must consult your own expert and find out the areas of agreement and disagreement between the experts. You will, of course, not cross-examine on the areas of agreement, but you must decide how you will cross-examine on the areas of disagreement. Your expert will help you. First, he will teach you everything you need to know about the subject of the expert's report and about which evidence will be given at trial.

In preparing your cross-examination of the expert keep the following points in mind:

1. Is the expert you are cross-examining really as expert in this field as your own expert? If not, bring out the lack of expertise in your cross-examination.
2. Is the expert's opinion contrary to that of recognized authority, and possibly contrary to the writings of the very expert you are cross-examining?
3. Most experts' opinions are based on certain factual assumptions. If these factual assumptions can be successfully attacked then the opinion will fail.
4. Bias.

It is often useful to have your expert sit beside you in court while the opposing expert is in the box. However, by this time you should no longer be in need of much assistance because of your preparation for the cross-examination. You will have reviewed your opposing expert's report with your own expert and will have obtained his oral and possibly even his written comments on the report. Your expert can help explain the evidence if this is necessary and can help you in your cross-examination. The mere fact of having your own expert sitting with you will often "tone down" the opposing expert's testimony, since he knows that there is someone very knowledgeable in his own field listening to him. You should, of course, ask the court's permission to have your expert sit at the counsel table.

Sometimes it is helpful to ask the expert witness whether he has submitted reports to counsel prior to the production of his final report and, if he has, seek production of the draft report or reports together with any letter by way of comment by counsel. If there is a change between the draft reports and the final report you will sometimes learn that this change was brought about following consultation with counsel. This will weaken the whole of the final report. Opposing counsel may well claim privilege, but I suggest that privilege is waived by production of the final report.

Often it is too dangerous to attack an expert head-on, and all you can do is circle around and get in a few nips here and there.

At the very least, when you are defending, you can qualify your own expert, who has not yet been called, through your cross-examination. Something like this:

Q. Dr. Smith, do you know Dr. Jones, Professor of Metallurgy at the University of Toronto?
A. Yes.
Q. I understand he is head of the department?
A. Yes.
Q. He is also the author of a number of articles and papers on this subject?
A. Yes.

Q. Is he not also the author of *Principles of Metallurgy?*
A. Yes.
Q. A standard text on the subject?
A. Yes.
Q. The problem we are dealing with today falls within his field of expertise?
A. Yes.
Q. You realize that I am calling him as a defence witness?
A. Yes.
Q. And you must agree that he is one of the leaders in his field on this continent?
A. Yes.

Do *not* go the next step and ask the question,

Q. You realize, of course, his opinion differs from yours?

because, although the answer will probably be Yes, he will try to explain the reason which will rebut your expert's opinion in advance.

If the expert's opinion is contrary to a recognized authority then face the expert with this inconsistency. This is how you do it:

Q. Dr. Smith, are you familiar with [the text and the author]?

You hope for and anticipate a Yes answer. If you get a No answer, it is well to point out to the witness that according to your information, which you will have to buttress by calling your own expert, this text is a standard text used in universities, etc.

A. Yes.
Q. I intend to read from page 56 of the text and will then ask you whether or not you agree with the statements there made.

At this point you hand a copy of the extract that you intend to read to your opponent and to the judge and then read the extract.

    Q. Do you agree with that statement?

Whether he answers Yes or No, go on:

    Q. Do you agree that the statement that I have just read to you is contrary to your opinion?
    A. Yes.

Again, do not ask him to explain and try not to let him explain.

You should, of course, have complete mastery of the facts, and particularly the facts upon which the expert has based his opinion. Sometimes it is possible to attack the foundation of the opinion by showing that the factual basis for the opinion was incorrect.

For example, take a case involving a back injury where the plaintiff claims a permanent disability, where the plaintiff told the doctor that prior to the accident he had never suffered from back pain and where you can prove a long history of complaints of back pain. The plaintiff's specialist has no knowledge of the pre-accident symptoms. Your cross-examination might be something like this:

    Q. Dr. Smith, you gave your opinion in direct examination that the present complaints of back pain are all due to the accident.
    A. Yes.
    Q. And you presumably based this opinion on the history given to you by the patient, that is, that the symptoms were initiated by the accident and that he suffered from no similar symptoms prior to the accident?
    A. Yes.

> Q. Your opinion, therefore, would be different if in fact
> Mr. Jones, the plaintiff, had complained of exactly the
> same symptoms for some years before the accident?
> A. Yes.

The cross-examination of expert witnesses is difficult, but
you can make a credible showing with thorough preparation
and by careful consultation with your own expert.

CHAPTER 22

RE-EXAMINATION

MANY COUNSEL SEEM to think that because they have the right to re-examine they should do so, because not to exercise this right would be to show weakness on their part. Nothing could be further from the truth. If you have thoroughly prepared your case and have covered all the relevant ground in your examination in chief there should be no need to re-examine since, with some exceptions, you may only re-examine on a new matter raised for the first time on cross-examination. You may not raise a completely new matter yourself.

Re-examination is a dangerous business. You are trying to rehabilitate a witness who has been knocked about in cross-examination. The witness is often feeling most unhappy about being a witness at all and just wants to get out of the witness box. There is a grave danger that re-examination will produce the same answers that he has just given in cross-examination and will substantially reinforce his harmful evidence.

Sometimes there is a serious inconsistency between what the witness said in chief and what he has just said in cross-examination. If you feel safe with the witness, you may wish to point out the inconsistency to him and ask for his explanation. If the inconsistency is only minor then do not take the risk. You draw the minor inconsistency to the attention of the court and risk a wrong answer.

As with examination in chief, you may not lead but you can,

of course, point the witness to the problem without suggesting the answer.

A good cross-examiner will keep the witness on a tight rein and will try to restrict the witness to Yes or No answers. If possible he will not permit the witness to explain. Sometimes it is clear to you that the witness wishes to explain his answer. This is particularly so with expert witnesses. On re-examination you can bring the witness back to his answer and ask for his explanation.

Occasionally a question is not fully answered and you can ask the witness whether there is anything he wants to add.

In a criminal trial, if the cross-examination has raised a suggestion of recent fabrication, you are permitted to re-examine to show an earlier consistent statement.

When part only of a conversation, or part only of a series of documents, has been cross-examined upon, you may wish to re-examine to bring out the rest of the conversation or the other documents.

The general rule, however, must be: only re-examine if you consider it really necessary.

CHAPTER 23

CLOSING

REMEMBER THAT IN the English-speaking provinces of Canada the great majority of judgments are delivered orally at the conclusion of argument or shortly thereafter. By this stage of the trial I suspect that most jurors have already reached a conclusion on liability. Now is the time to put it all together and produce certainty. With a judge alone you want to help him organize his reasons for judgment, and with a jury you want to give them the specific answers to the questions that will be left with them.

Just as in your opening address, it is improper to give your personal opinion. You are an advocate and you make submissions.

The attention span of a jury, and even of a judge, is limited. In an ordinary case a closing address of one hour is much too long. With a jury you need to take a little longer than with a judge, but you should be able to make your points and still keep their attention within 30 to 45 minutes. We are told that Abraham Lincoln's jury addresses seldom lasted longer than 20 minutes.[1]

Be courteous, sincere, logical and do not move about the court room.

You have worked out the theory of your case from when

---

[1]Francis L. Wellman, *Day in Court* (N.Y., Macmillan, 1910), pp. 245-6.

you first completed your investigation of the facts and long before trial. This theory should show through the whole trial and into your closing address.

Often in a trial there is a short piece of vital evidence. It is helpful to get the court reporter to transcribe this evidence for you so that you can read the verbatim extract to the court. With a judge alone you can hand him or her a copy. Most court reporters have a good relationship with "their judge", and if asked to transcribe some evidence will tell the judge and will often provide the judge with a copy. This, of course, can be helpful to you.

Closing to a judge alone

Do not weakly drop your case in the judge's lap: "Your Lordship has heard all of the evidence and I am in your hands." Your client deserves more than this. Organize your argument in the same basic order that the judge will use in delivering reasons for judgment. The judge in delivering reasons will isolate the issues, review the facts, make any necessary findings of fact and credibility, apply the law to the facts and reach a conclusion.

It is helpful to prepare an outline of your argument. Do not read your argument; the outline will serve as your note. It may also be helpful to hand a copy of your outline to the judge; it may be helpful in organizing his or her reasons and will certainly impress him or her with your preparation.

Generally speaking your outline should follow this order:

(1)   the issues and your position on the issues;
(2)   a brief summary of the evidence on each issue with any necessary findings of fact;

(3) the applicable law on each issue;

(4) the conclusion on each issue and the relief claimed.

Very often there is only one issue in the case. In a complicated case there may be two, or even three, but seldom more.

You will often have to deal with the credibility of witnesses. In making your submission on credibility consider the following:

(1) which version is more inherently probable;

(2) the fact that the evidence of your witness was not shaken on cross-examination;

(3) the fact that the evidence of your witness was supported by contemporaneous notes or by documentary evidence;

(4) inconsistencies in the evidence opposed to the evidence of your witnesses; and

(5) bias.

After dealing with credibility, ask the judge to make a specific finding of credibility and specific findings of fact. You may not get these findings, but he that does not ask gets no answer. Even if you sense that the trial judge will in the result find against you on the legal result of the facts as found, you may well obtain findings of fact in your client's favour that will assist you in the Court of Appeal should that court take a different view of the law.

You should have already handed in your brief of law. The brief will be divided into sections corresponding with the listed issues. You do not need many authorities on each issue. You do need the pertinent sections of the relevant Act or regulations, an extract from a recognized text and one or two recent decisions. Make sure your recent decisions have not been reversed or modified on appeal. I once heard counsel refer to a Court of Appeal decision in the Supreme Court of Canada only to be advised by the Chief Justice that the decision had been reversed in that court two weeks before.

If you do not hand in a note of argument then outline your issues and points in argument slowly so that the judge can note them. In a long complicated case you may need to review the evidence in some detail — your chronology will help (see Chapter 18).

Do not be afraid of questions from the Bench. It shows you the way the judge is thinking and helps you to make your argument fit the judge's train of thought or solve his or her problem. Try to deal with the question at once and then get back to the order of your argument.

Try to make it easy for the judge to make a decision. In some cases, if certain findings of fact are made, it will not be necessary to deal with certain troublesome legal problems. Show the judge the way.

Closing to a jury

Your task of persuasion is the same but your audience is less experienced in decision-making. Your case is usually simpler and turns on the facts. You are permitted to tell the jury some basic legal propositions so that your submissions can be properly understood — for example the onus in a pedestrian case and the burden of proof in a criminal trial — but generally speaking you may not instruct them in the law.

In most civil cases the jury makes its decision by answering a series of written questions. Always ask the judge to fix the questions before you make your closing address. The whole thrust of your argument is to get the answer or answers that will win the case. It is sometimes helpful during your jury address to take a black felt marker and actually write in the answers that you want on the copy of the question sheet and show these answers to the jury.

Be sincere, straightforward and fair. Do not talk down to the jury: use simple language and maintain "eye contact". I think it a mistake to call the jury "folk" or "guys". They are "members of the jury" or "ladies and gentlemen of the jury".

I will end with a true story. It is not unusual, and quite proper when there are more than one counsel in the same interest, for counsel, with the permission of the judge, to leave the court room from time to time during the trial and let counsel in the same interest look after the shop. It is most unusual for a judge to do so.

A Supreme Court Judge, who is no longer with us, did exactly this in a civil jury trial in which I was involved. He had charged the jury but became impatient when hours went by with no verdict, particularly since he had a plane to catch for the South. An accommodating brother judge agreed to take the jury verdict, only to have the jury knock and ask a complicated question. With the assistance of counsel the question was duly answered and a verdict delivered with no appeal, but I will never forget the look on the faces of the jurors when they came in to see a different judge on the Bench!

INDEX